AWAKENING THE CHAKRAS THROUGH YOGA

AWAKENING THE CHAKRAS THROUGH YOGA

Claire Rodgers
Mamta Kanabar

KALPAZ

ISBN: 978-81-7835-992-2

Price : ₹ 485

First Published 2013

Published by

Kalpaz Publications
C-30, Satyawati Nagar,
Delhi - 110052
E-mail: kalpaz@hotmail.com Ph.: 9212142040

Laser Typesetting : Rajender Vashist, Delhi
Photographers: Kabir Kanabar and Vinny Rooney
Printed at : G. Print Process, Delhi

Cataloging in Publication Data--DK
Courtesy: D.K. Agencies (P) Ltd. <docinfo@dkagencies.com>

Kanabar, Mamta.
Awakening the chakras through yoga / Mamta Kanabar, Claire Rodgers.
p. cm.
Includes index.
ISBN 9788178359922

1. Chakras. 2. Yoga. I. Rodgers, Claire, joint author. II. Title.

DDC 131 23

Mamta and Claire would like to dedicate this book to the yoga teachers, they have had the privilege to learn from and to their yoga students, who they have had the privilege to teach

Contents

Introduction

Yoga is an ancient tradition derived from India, thought to be thousands of years old. In recent decades it has become a widely practiced approach to improve health and well-being in both East and West. In many forms of yoga, particularly those more popular in the West, it is often the physical postures and exercises known as *asanas* which are given more prominence. In comparison, more traditional approaches to yoga often place equal or greater emphasis on working with the breath, through the practice of *pranayama* and working with energy and consciousness through the yoga practices of bandha, *mudra*, *mantra* and meditation.

It is precisely these practices which make yoga so different from other physical exercise systems. Its focus not only on the physical body, but also the breath, the mind and the energy body, make it a unique and powerful system of healing which is truly holistic in nature.

We often experience ourselves as a sum of parts, rather than as a whole being and it is here that yoga can be most effective. Meaning to 'yoke' or come together, yoga is essentially about integration, the coming together of mind, body and spirit. Its practice encourages us to be present within our body, to be focused on our breath, to be aware of the workings of the mind without being controlled by our thoughts and to tune into and accept, rather than repress, our emotions. In doing so we become less distracted by mental chatter and are more able to observe the more subtle aspects of our being.

As we progress in our yoga practice we can develop awareness of the subtle body, known as the energy body and its' energy centres, known as the chakras. As we learn how these energy centres play a vital role in our physical, emotional and psychological health and how their qualities manifest in our thoughts, feelings and behaviour, we can identify where there may be imbalance in the energy of the chakras. Through yoga, meditation, positive affirmation and visualisation, we can consciously awaken and re-balance our energy and in doing so, give ourselves the great gift of self-healing.

With regular practice yoga can bring not only improved health, strength and flexibility to the physical body, but also greater clarity of mind, increased levels of energy and vitality and a growing sense of inner peace and happiness which help sustain us through the sometimes turbulent times we encounter in life. Over time, yoga not only brings integration of the different aspects of our being, but also becomes something we assimilate into our daily life, informing how we live and how we relate to ourselves, other people and the world around us.

1

The Energy Body

Although familiar with energy levels being low when we are fatigued or high when we feel strong and vigorous, the concept of an energy body can seem alien or at best irrelevant, as it is something most of us don't directly experience. In Western models of health and medicine, emphasis is placed on the physical body and on diagnosing and treating the physical symptoms of ill-health or disease. Eastern models of health tend to focus instead on the detection of underlying imbalances in the energy system within the body and seek to restore balance and so prevent physical ill-health. In Eastern approaches to medicine, it is thought that the energy field of the body first exhibits imbalance and if left unattended, this imbalance may then manifest at a physical or psychological level.

The energy body is thought to be the link between our physical body and our consciousness. Our emotions, beliefs and habitual ways of thinking which we develop in response to our experiences in life are reflected in our energy system. When we are unable to integrate and accept parts of our emotional experiences, they are held as tension within the energy body and if we are unable to process or release this tension, it may then emerge as a physical or psychological symptom, where the body shows us that there is something we are not dealing with. If we continue to ignore this communication from the body, the symptom may develop into something more severe or can manifest as a chronic illness.

Just as we have our own unique, individual consciousness

and an energy body reflecting this, there is also thought to be a universal consciousness and universal energy field, of which we are part. This universal energy, known as *Prana* in yoga, as Chi or Qi in Chinese medicine and as Ki in Japanese healing, is contained in the air and permeates all life. Energy is in fact all that there is, constantly flowing, it vibrates or resonates at different frequencies, giving the appearance of dense, physical matter when its vibration is slow.

Prana is derived from the Sanskrit verb 'pru', meaning to fill and 'na' meaning all around. *Prana* is all pervading and carries the dynamic properties of *Prakriti*, in yoga philosophy, the energy of creation. Intertwined with *Prakriti* is *Purusha*, pure consciousness, the witness to the energy of creation. *Prakriti* is thought to have the potential for transformation, but no ability to move or transform on its own as it has no consciousness. It is only through coming together with the passive, observing consciousness of *Purusha* that it can create. *Prakriti* and *Purusha* are thought to be infinite and eternal forms of energy and only through their intertwining can the universe become manifest.

Prana is the energy which allows matter to have life, movement and vitality. It flows within every single cell, fills all that exists and is absorbed through the breath, through sunlight, fresh water and food and through the earth beneath us. A good diet and plenty of fresh air are known to be important in maintaining good health, but many of us don't realise the importance of how we breathe. Breathing well, using the full capacity of the lungs, not only allows us to increase the levels of oxygen in the body and more effectively rid the body of waste products but also allows more *prana* to be absorbed. Contained within *prana* are different types of energy associated with particular functions, such as absorption, elimination and distribution of energy through the body. Each of these types of energy is governed within a particular energy centre within the energy body and each of these functions are aligned with the rhythm of the breath; the inhalation, which absorbs and takes in; the exhalation, which eliminates and expels and the pause between the two, which disperses and circulates the breath. The breath and the *prana* it carries work in unity within the physical and energy body, drawing in, distributing and releasing the essential nutrients, waste products and energy we need to live and thrive.

When our thoughts, beliefs and emotions are negative, we hold tension in the energy body and this reflects in how we hold ourselves physically. We close off and shut down areas of the body where this tension is held, keeping it out of our awareness. As a result we develop tight muscles and poor posture which not only constrict the internal organs, but also inhibit our breathing, making it shallow and imbalanced, impeding the absorption of *prana* via the breath. As we close off areas of the body we not only reduce the amount of *prana* we can absorb, but also restrict its' flow, causing it to stagnate. Our life force, our energy 'spark' within becomes depleted, our energy becomes sluggish and this dullness is reflected not only in the body, but also in the mind. A downward spiral of negativity, tension, poor posture, shallow, imbalanced breath and depleted, restricted *prana* develops. We become unhappy, lacking in energy, our health suffers and we become unable to live our life fully or to fulfil our true potential.

This is where the great gift of yoga can become our saving grace. The physical poses or *asanas* work on opening and strengthening the body, allowing muscles to release, posture to improve and more space to be created for the breath. Breathing consciously and more effectively enhances the space within the body, not only allowing more *prana* to be absorbed but also allowing it to flow more easily, carried to all of the internal organs and to every cell within us, creating a vibrant body, filled with the universal life-force. Specific breathing exercises can help us to direct *prana* to particular parts of the body which we may want to energise and can also be employed to have a vitalising or calming effect on the mind.

As *prana* begins to flow more freely through the body, we can open and discharge the blockages, tensions and constrictions within the energy body, releasing areas of stagnant energy and letting go of the negativity and fear we have repressed. By staying present within the body and focused on the breath as we practice, our emotions are able to be accepted and integrated rather than stifled and pushed out of our awareness. Being present with body and breath also allows us to observe rather than identify with, the workings of the mind. The mind becomes something we witness and with practice, a tool through which we study ourselves and are slowly able to discern which thoughts and beliefs create fear and tension and which create more positive and helpful experiences. As self-awareness develops, we can consciously let go of critical, fear-based thoughts and replace with positive, affirming and hopeful thoughts. As we continue to progress in our yoga practice, our energy becomes balanced and clear, our physical body healthy and strong, our mind hopeful and happy.

Within the energy body, *prana* is understood to flow through channels, known as *nadis*, meaning 'flow', or 'stream'. These channels, numbering around 72,000, correspond with the network of nerve channels, which we know as the nervous system of the physical body. Within the *nadis* flows our consciousness, the impressions from our senses and experiences in life and within the nerve channels flows our reactions to our experiences. The three major *nadis*, known as *Sushumna*, *Ida* and *Pingala* in yoga philosophy, correspond with the spinal cord, the central channel of the nervous system. *Sushumna* is the central energy channel with *Ida* and *Pingala* originating on the left and right sides of *Sushumna* at the base of the spine.

Ida is associated with energy more female in its nature, introverted and reflective and linked to the energy of the moon. *Pingala* is associated with energy more male in its nature, outgoing and active and linked to the energy of the sun. These major *nadis* reflect the contrasting forces within us. At any one time, one or other of the two channels is dominant and only when they are equally balanced does energy begin to flow in the central *nadi*, *Sushumna*, when the mind is still and we are in a meditative state. By checking which nostril is breathing more strongly we can identify which *nadi* is active. When the breath flows more strongly in the right nostril, *Pingala* is dominant and we are ready for more energetic and physical activity. With the left more dominant, *Ida* is active and we are more suited to slow down and to focus on mental undertakings. The flow is thought to alternate between the two every ninety minutes or so and serves to regulate the energy of the body and mind throughout the day. The ancient science of *Swara* yoga precisely monitors the flow and quality of breath in each nostril and connects this not only to the kinds of activities best suited to perform according to the breath flow, but also to the position of the moon, the planets and the seasons. By balancing the flow of the breath and the action of the major *nadis* with the wider energy of the cosmos, greater harmony between our individual energy and the energy of the universe is created.

These two major *nadis* also correspond to the sympathetic and para-sympathetic nervous systems. *Pingala* corresponds to the sympathetic, predominantly controlled by the left hemisphere of the brain, allowing us to energise and stimulate the physical body, *Ida* to the para-sympathetic, predominantly controlled by the right hemisphere of the brain, allowing us to slow down and relax. As the diaphragm is the only muscle which connects to both the sympathetic and para-sympathetic nervous systems and is integral to how we breathe, we can see once more how the breath is central to balancing our energy and exists as the bridge between body, mind and spirit.

Ida's properties are very much aligned with the functions of the right hemisphere of the brain, which controls the left side of the body and *Pingala's* with the left hemisphere, controlling the right side of the body. Right and left hemisphere functions and *Ida* and *Pingala* associated qualities are shown in the table below.

Right hemisphere	*Ida Properties*	*Left Hemisphere*	*Pingala Properties*
Insightful	Feminine	Logical	Masculine
Creative	Emotional	Rational	Analytical
Subjective	Day-dreaming	Objective	Activity
Symbolic	Cool	Practical	Warm
Artistic	Inward-looking	Scientific	Outward-looking
Whole Picture	Moon	Categories	Sun
Non-verbal	Holistic	Verbal	Methodical

As *Ida* and *Pingala* travel upwards from the base of the spine, they form a double helix shape which intersects at various points along *Sushumna*. At the intersection of these points lie the chakras, the main energy centres of the body. Although there are many minor chakras, such as those in the hands, the seven major chakras have the most influence over body and mind. Each one is concerned with a different aspect of our consciousness, reflecting how we relate to ourselves, others and the world around us.

By understanding the qualities associated with each chakra and how these qualities may manifest within our body, our thoughts and behaviours, we can identify which areas in our life may be most unbalanced. We can then work to consciously awaken and balance the energy of each chakra and so improve the health of the body and mind. As we purify the energy centres and the *nadis*, our energy can flow freely, we can learn to focus the mind and prepare ourselves for meditation. In meditation, the dormant energy of *kundalini* which is thought to reside in the base chakra and represents our true power and potential as spiritual beings, can begin to rise in *Sushumna nadi*. With regular, steady practice, *kundalini* reaches the crown chakra at the top of the head and we connect our individual consciousness to universal consciousness, experiencing the absolute peace and joy of this higher, universal force.

2

The Chakras and the Energy Body

The chakras correspond not only with the intersection of *Ida* and *Pingala*, along the central energy channel *Sushumna*, but also at the points where many of the *nadis* from the periphery of the energy body intersect. The chakras are like whirlpools of energy, drawing energy in from all over the body and then processing, balancing and re-distributing this energy back out into the *nadis*. The chakras also correspond with the position of nerve plexuses or networks of nerves from the peripheral nervous system, located along the spinal cord and with the position of the main glands within the body. It would make sense therefore that the subtle or energy body and what we understand as the physical body (though this is also energy, just vibrating at a slower rate), inter-relate through both the glandular, or endocrine system and the nervous system.

There are seven main chakras. The first is *Mooladhara*, the base chakra, located at the base of the body. The second is *Swadhistana*, the sacral chakra, located in the lower abdomen. The third is *Manipura*, the solar plexus chakra, located in the belly. The fourth is *Anahata*, the heart chakra, located in the heart. The fifth is *Vishuddhi*, the throat chakra, located in the throat. The sixth is *Ajna*, the third eye chakra, located in the forehead and the seventh is *Sahasrara*, the crown chakra, located in the top of the head. The chakras are symbolised as geometric patterns known as *yantras*, which reflect their particular energy. Each *yantra* has both a lotus flower and a Sanskrit letter symbolising the associated sound vibration of the *mantra* which resonates at the same vibration as its corresponding chakra, known as the *bija* or source *mantra*. The lotus flower represents our spiritual journey from the mud of the earth, through the water, to the sun and sky above, as our energy rises from base to crown chakra and we grow from spiritual ignorance to wisdom and bliss. Each lotus flower also has a specific number of petals which represent the main *nadis* which connect to the chakra.

The chakras reflect different aspects of our consciousness and also act as antennae, allowing us to tune into the energy field surrounding us and to sense the energy of other people. We send out our own energy too, so are transmitting and receiving energy at an unconscious level, communicating with others without consciously knowing. When we become more aware of our energy body we begin to develop greater awareness of this unconscious communication and can pick up on, not only the body language of others, but also tune into the quality of their energy and the energy we may or may not be sending out. We acquire more of a 'feel' about people and places. This greater awareness not only brings valuable insight into our relationships, but also allows us to become more attuned to the universal energy surrounding us, more in sync with the rhythm of life itself.

All of life is permeated by energy and that energy comes into being through the elements, known as the *tattwas*, translating as 'that' which is within all. Within the *tattwas* are the building blocks of all existence, known as the *gunas* or ropes of existence, which are the dynamic aspect of life itself. The *gunas* are properties of *Prakriti*, the element of creation, which is carried within *prana*. They are known as *raja*; activity or movement, *tamas*; darkness and denseness, and *sattva*; harmony, where clarity and light is found. The *gunas* are constantly intertwining and interweaving in an on-going cosmic dance, never mixing with each other, but reacting towards and against each other. They are the threads which make up all matter in the natural world, in constant dynamic interplay. In yoga philosophy the *gunas* were thought to be in a perfect state of equilibrium when the universe came into being, with the 'big bang'. The energy and vibration released through this perfect state caused *Prakriti* to manifest, and through its interaction with pure consciousness, *Purusha*, the universe could evolve. Before the big bang, *Prakriti* and *Purusha*, eternal and infinite, existed, but in an un-manifest form.

We are accustomed to thinking of physical matter as the first to evolve from the beginnings of the universe, but the ancient *yogis* profess that the first to evolve was '*buddhi*', the higher mind or intellect. *Buddhi* is thought to evolve from sattva, when *Prakriti* on seeing its reflection in the clarity and light of *sattva*, mistakes this as its true identity and not merely a reflection. From here the true self, the eternal, pure consciousness is overlooked and the reflection becomes the 'Self'. From *buddhi* emerges the sense of separateness, the ego, or 'I am', known as *ahamkara*, the 'I-maker'. From *ahamkara*, the subtle aspects of the senses emerge; sound, taste, touch, sight and smell, and from these, the five main elements or *tattwas*. Space, the most subtle of energetic vibrations is the first *tattwa* to emerge. From space comes air, from air comes fire, from fire comes water and from water, earth. From the elements, the senses evolve, through which we experience the physical world. So, our reality becomes our perception of the world experienced by the self or ego through the senses, and we begin to attach ourselves and our identity to our perceptions, continually projecting ourselves outwards, rather than realising the true self, the pure consciousness within.

The five *tattwas* are housed within the five lower chakras and each of the five senses is influenced by a particular chakra. *Buddhi* is housed within the sixth chakra and the seventh chakra, our gateway to universal consciousness, transcends the elements. The energy of each chakra vibrates at a particular frequency and corresponds with the colour which vibrates at that same frequency. The colour of the chakra reflects the physical, emotional and spiritual state of that aspect of our consciousness connected to the chakra. So the colour can be bright and shining, radiating with pure colour, or dull and muddied, with the colour barely discernible, reflecting the qualities of our thoughts and emotions. Similarly, the energy of the chakra can spin evenly and smoothly or have a jagged, irregular movement, again reflecting our state of mind. The chakra can become blocked if we suffer trauma, fear or stress or can be too open, when our personal boundaries are damaged and we become unable to protect ourselves from other people's energy. By directing our consciousness to the chakra, using breathing exercises, meditation, positive visualisation and affirmation, we can clear, purify and balance the flow of its energy.

Surrounding the body are five vibrational bodies or layers of energy, often called the aura. The layers of vibration are known as the *mayakoshas* and translate as the *koshas* or sheaths, which give the appearance of covering or veiling (*maya*) the true self or pure consciousness within. The energy of the chakras is denser than the *mayakoshas* and more rooted within the body. Like the chakras, the *mayakoshas* store impressions and vibrations from different aspects of our being, though are more changeable and reflect our moods more easily, with the aura usually having a dominant colour, reflecting which aspect of ourself is more dominant at any one time. The aura can be weak and thin when we are anxious and fearful or expansive and strong when we are confident and self-assured. We can perceive the aura of others and pick up on the quality of their energy, so our reaction to others is often a reflection of their energy field connecting with, or intruding into, our own. As we awaken, strengthen and balance the energy of the chakras through our yoga and meditation practices the aura also becomes strengthened and bright.

Like the five lower chakras each *mayakosha* houses one of the five elements and like the chakras each has its own particular vibration, with the base chakra and the *annamayakosha* (known as the food body) vibrating at a slower rate than the others. As the chakras move upwards and the *mayakoshas* move from layer to layer the rate of vibration is faster. *Annamayakosha* houses the earth element and reflects the health of the physical body; *pranamayakosha* houses the water element and reflects the health of the breath; *manamayakosha* houses the fire element and reflects the health of manas, the lower mind, our thoughts and beliefs;

vijnamayakosha houses the air element and reflects the health of the higher mind, our wisdom, and *anandamayakosha*, which houses space and is known as the bliss body is thought to cover the inner true self of pure consciousness. Like the chakras each *mayakosha* affects the others around it. Together with the *tattwas*, the chakras, *nadis* and *mayakoshas* form a holistic energetic system. They are our unique energy body, surrounding us yet also permeating every living cell within us, reflecting every aspect of our being and connecting us to the universal energy encompassing all.

Where the major energy channels, *Ida* and *Pingala* intersect along the central channel *Sushumna*, one or other is more dominant and the corresponding chakra reflects more of the qualities of the dominant *nadi*. The base, solar plexus and throat chakras for instance are associated with how we actively express our energy to the world, how we assert ourselves and communicate to those around us, reflecting the outward-looking energy of *Pingala nadi*. The sacral, heart and third eye chakras reflect the more inward-looking qualities of *Ida*, such as our creativity, love and intuition. Each chakra is also linked to an associated gland and affects not only the corresponding area of the physical body, but also the functioning of that gland. *Ida* and *Pingala* meet at the third eye chakra, the chakra most associated with the mind and there are specific breathing practices for this chakra which help to balance the right and left hemispheres of the brain and purify and balance *Ida* and *Pingala nadis*, preparing body, mind and energy for the practice of meditation. At *Sahasrara*, the crown chakra, our perception of duality, of the contrasting forces within us; male and female, left and right; emotion and logic, are transcended. It is also here that we unite with pure consciousness, transcending the illusion of ourselves as separate beings and becoming one with universal energy.

The chakras are connected to different aspects of our consciousness, so play an integral role in linking the body and mind. They are thought to develop as we do, reflecting our emotions and experiences as we grow from womb to early adulthood. Each chakra therefore corresponds to a particular stage of our development and throughout adulthood, the thoughts and fears we experience which resonate with that stage of development will be stored within or around the associated chakra, affecting its vibrancy and strength.

Our base chakra reflects our experiences from womb to babyhood and is linked to our physical security and to what extent we can trust the world to look after us, reflecting our need for nurturing and safety when we are so vulnerable and dependant. The sacral chakra reflects our infancy, when we begin to explore the world and take our first tentative steps to autonomy, including becoming aware of our body and beginning toilet training. If encouraged and allowed to explore, we can enjoy the world, becoming creative and curious, but if criticised or overly-controlled, we feel guilt and shame. The solar plexus reflects our early childhood from two to five years where we begin to assert our will, develop initiative and test our boundaries and our power. If we are thwarted and squashed we fear asserting ourselves and mistrust our power and if given too much control and power, without understanding ourselves, we can become 'little tyrants' and continue to expect to dominate and have our own way throughout life. The heart chakra reflects middle childhood, from five to eight years where we develop competence and self-love and are encouraged to make our own friendships and begin to understand our feelings and our relationships with others. If we are able to do so, we feel confident and hopeful, if thwarted we feel inferior and undeserving of love. The throat chakra reflects our development from eight to twelve years and is where we begin to express ourselves as individuals, making our voice heard as we become more independent. If encouraged, we are confident and able to express our essence and truth, if thwarted, we deny our truth and are fearful of its expression. The brow chakra reflects our teenage years where we develop our sense of identity, a clear picture of who we are and the role we might take in life. If we can do so, we trust ourselves and become more able to follow our intuition, if we cannot, we may become confused and unable to find our path in life. In adulthood, the crown chakra reflects to what extent we can live our life with integrity, how we have assimilated the experiences of our early years, or whether we continue to feel unsettled and unsure, repressing and denying aspects of ourselves. By awakening and balancing each chakra we can process, accept and integrate our formative experiences.

For many of us, the body and mind are viewed as separate entities and we rarely experience the physical, mental and energetic body as an integrated whole. We may make little connection to the role of our emotions, our thoughts or how our energy system is functioning when there are physical problems. Similarly, we take little notice of our emotional and mental health and the potential link to our physical health or to our energy body. Many of us live our lives with little exercise, a diet overloaded with processed food lacking in essential nutrients and natural *prana*, poor posture, limited breath capacity and habitually negative beliefs and thoughts. Our energy system will reflect this. When we envisage energy as light, we can imagine how bright, clear, shining light flowing unobstructed through the body will bring us vibrancy and health, like a clear, sparkling mountain stream, surrounded by blue sky, in harmony with all around. By slowly and steadily working through the yoga practices, we allow the energy body and the chakras to awaken, to flow freely and to function as one whole system, each chakra in harmony with the others and with the energy surrounding us. In doing so, our health and happiness improve, and we become more able to fulfil our potential and lead fuller and more joyful lives.

3

The Chakras and the Physical Body

The body has an amazing capacity to restore balance, to repair and heal itself and the many factors affecting the healing process are often not fully understood. Key to fighting infection and defending against parasites or mutations is the immune system. Working closely with this is the endocrine or hormonal system, which regulates the body via the production and release of hormones. The glands of the endocrine system detect changes in the body and when signalled by the brain via the nervous system, will release and sometimes produce hormones. These are secreted into the bloodstream causing various chemical and bio-chemical reactions which seek to restore equilibrium. Through the study of endocrinology, modern medicine has made huge advances in understanding the function of the glands in relation to the health of the body. The glands however, have a dual function, in that they also sense imbalance in vibrational energy and in so doing, along with the nervous system, act as the communicators between the physical body and the energy body.

In the physical body, the gland located in the centre of the head which produces melotonin and serotonin and is thought to regulate sleep rhythms and mood is the pineal gland. In yoga, the corresponding energy centre located at the top of the head is *Sahasrara* which is associated with higher states of consciousness and transcendence of the physical body, through deep meditation. The slow brainwaves observed in deep sleep, known as delta waves are the same brainwaves observed within deep meditative states when the meditator is still conscious, so the gland and the chakra are regulating our levels of consciousness, through sleep, when we are unconscious and through meditation when we are conscious. The function of the delta waves and their role in sleep is little understood. The pineal gland together with the pituitary, are thought to be the master glands of the body and the pineal is described by Descartes as 'the seat of the soul'. Through *Sahasrara*, it is thought that the universal life-force enters the system and through its connection to the pineal gland allows the life-force to be distributed through the energy body and our mood and energy levels to be regulated. Through the practices of yoga and meditation our connection to this life-force can be strengthened and so our ability to transcend the purely physical plane of existence and to connect with what is beyond our normal level of perception, to a higher, more spiritual realm is heightened.

Once thought of as the master gland, the pituitary is now known to have some of its functions regulated by the pineal gland. In a similar way to the glandular system, the chakras have a hierarchical though not entirely linear 'command' structure. For the chakras, this hierarchy is linked to realms of consciousness, with the higher chakras of *Ajna* and *Sahasrara* associated with higher states of consciousness and the lower chakras concerned more with our relationships, our sense of self and our survival in the physical world. In meditation, gamma brainwaves, which are much faster than delta brainwaves have also been observed. They are observed when the mind becomes completely focused and they work to actually change the pre-frontal cortex, causing fear and anxiety to decrease and happiness, acceptance and feelings of compassion to increase. The pre-frontal cortex is located in the same place as *ajna* chakra and the gamma waves observed within the brain, in people who have a regular meditation practice, appear to sweep through the whole brain, allowing not only integration and more connection between its different parts, but also improved memory, concentration and intelligence. *Ajna* chakra, the energy centre associated with the higher functions of the mind, with intuition, wisdom and self-unity appears to mirror the function of these gamma waves. The pituitary gland has many functions, regulates a range of hormones and is linked to many bodily systems. It makes sense therefore, that a gland with such an overall link to regulating the many systems of the body and presiding over the innate wisdom of the body is connected to the chakra concerned with the conscious qualities of wisdom, intuition and unity.

As we travel down the body, the next major glands are the thyroid and para-thyroid glands, important in hormone secretions linked to the regulation of energy in cells, in turn governing our metabolism and nerve function. These glands, situated in the base of the throat are thought to correspond to the energy centre of *Vishuddhi* chakra, linked to our knowledge of self and expression of being. *Vishuddhi* is also thought to be concerned with being open to life, to our communication and our ability to teach and transmit the wisdom we receive from the higher energy centres. Given the connection of the thyroid gland to metabolism and to nervous system functioning, expression of self and how we communicate to others, makes sense as the main function of *Vishuddhi* chakra, as people are often described or perceived in ways which reflect their energy e.g. 'quick', 'plodding' 'lethargic', 'dull', 'easy-going' or 'edgy'.

The thymus gland, associated with the heart and located as two separate lobes above and in contact with the heart, is particularly active during development of the foetus and in establishing the immune system in the early years of childhood. The heart chakra, *Anahata* is located in the heart centre and associated with love, compassion, ambition and hope. It is linked to the plane of consciousness concerned with loving of, and beyond the self. The link between the heart centre and immune system is significant when we consider recent developments in the field of psycho-immunology. Strengthening the immune system through positive thoughts, visualisation and affirmations around self-love and hope are now looked on as significant in the treatment of many conditions and appear to connect the immune system to the functions of its energy centre, *Anahata*.

Further down the physical body is the energy centre known as *Manipura* chakra, the solar plexus, located in the belly and associated with our sense of self. It is linked to our willingness and ability to re-claim personal power, to digest experience, learn and grow from this experience, and ultimately, transform. Likened to the energy of fire, its' energy is concerned with whether and how, we 'rise from the ashes' of life's experiences. This digestion of experience and our associated 'gut' reactions and responses, links well with the pancreas, the gland so essential to the balanced functioning of the digestive system in the physical body. Without our digestive system functioning well, we are unable to draw nurture from our food and the *prana* contained within it and so the whole body becomes weakened. Similarly, without processing and integrating our emotional reactions to our experiences in life, we can weaken our energy by repressing and avoiding our feelings.

In the lower abdomen we find the sexual and reproductive glands, the ovaries and testes, linked to fertility, reproduction and sexual energy. *Swadhisthana*, the associated chakra is linked to creativity, to the element of water and with the flow of any liquid through the body. In terms of consciousness, its' energy is expressed as our ability to create, to give birth to new concepts and ideas and to navigate and flow through life. It is also linked to expression of our inner selves and emotions through our sexuality and creativity, so mirrors the physical functions of its associated glands. When we accept ourselves as creative, sexual beings, we can let go of the shame and guilt so commonly attached to sex and allow ourselves to take pleasure and enjoyment from life, becoming fulfilled and happy in the process.

At the base of the body is *Mooladhara* chakra, the root chakra. This energy centre is thought to be concerned with our connection to the physical plane of existence, to earth energy, our physical needs, our survival and security. It is associated with the adrenal glands situated on the top of each kidney and responsible for the production of adrenalin and nor-adrenalin, governing the 'fight or flight' survival mechanism. *Mooladhara* is central to our ability to feel grounded and calm, just as the adrenals are central to expressing how anxious and fearful, or how safe and secure we feel. When balanced, *Mooladhara* gives us the secure base from which we can grow.

As we work with the chakras, we can see a progression from the lower chakras concerned with our physical survival, our relationships and our sense of self, to the higher chakras associated with love, expression and wisdom and ultimately to inter-connectedness and awareness of higher planes of consciousness. As we awaken and re-balance the energy of each chakra, the glandular and the nervous systems also become more balanced and the health of our whole being, body, mind and spirit improves.

4

The Practices

Working with Postures and Breath

The yoga *asanas* work to improve our posture, lengthen and strengthen the muscles and bring more flexibility and stamina to the body. When this happens our organs are less likely to be constricted by tension and tightness in the muscular-skeletal system and become positioned in the body more openly. They can then more effectively receive the oxygen, nutrients and energy they require. The importance given to the breath in the practice of yoga is one of its central features. Breathing effectively allows us to increase the supply of oxygen as well as *prana*, to the body and to expel waste and toxins from the body. This is essential for optimal functioning of the endocrine, nervous and circulatory systems and for our organs, particularly the brain, to receive a healthy supply of essential nutrients. Awareness of the quality of our breath, observation of changes in our breath and focusing on where we direct the breath within the body allows us to experience the yoga *asanas* more fully and to more effectively reap their benefits.

Pranayama, the science of yoga breathing, allows control of the *prana* contained within the breath and employs specific breathing practices to further benefit the health of the physical body, soothe the nervous system and help us both develop awareness of, and stimulate, the energy of the chakras. There are many *pranayama* practices, some involving prolonging the inhale and/or exhale, quickening the breath, closing the right or left nostril, or pausing and holding the breath after inhalation or exhalation. In addition, the breath can be directed or held within particular parts of the body, after inhale or exhale, allowing areas of the body to be charged with energy. These practices can be used with *pranayama* or with *asana* and are known as bandhas or energy locks. The three main *bandhas*, *moola bandha*, *uddiyana bandha* and *jalandara bandha* work on their own, directing energy to particular areas of the body or can be employed together for greater intensity.

Pranayama can be used to improve balance between the brain hemispheres and the *Ida* and *Pingala* energy channels, by directing the breath into the right or left nostril. It can be employed to pacify, cool or soothe the mind and body or to increase heat and vitality within the body. In the chakra chapters (chapters 8 to 15) those breathing practices and bandhas which work more effectively to awaken each particular chakra shall be outlined.

The practice of *asana* and *pranayama* allows us to focus the mind and attention on the breath and so allows us to begin to withdraw our awareness from the distractions perceived by our senses. Withdrawal from these distractions is known as *Pratyahara*. It is the beginning of a concentrated or one-pointed mind, known as *Dharana*, which prepares us for *Dhyana*, the meditative state, where we experience oneness with the focus of our meditation and which ultimately leads us to the blissful state of *Samadhi*, where we connect with pure consciousness. These practices, together with moral restraints and observances, known as the *Yamas* and *Niyamas* (outlined in the following chapter) form the eight-fold path to enlightenment which was outlined by the great yogic sage *Patanjali*.

Working with *Mudra*, *Mantra* and Meditation

Mudras, *mantras*, and meditation, combined with *asana* and *pranayama*, seek to re-balance our energy body and ultimately allow us to observe rather than identify with and be controlled by, the workings of the mind. Through practice, the benefits can then begin to be experienced in day to day life as we become more aware of and attuned to the workings of the body, breath and mind and ultimately to the development of harmony within and between, the physical, mental and energetic systems of the body.

In *mudra*, meaning gesture or seal of energy, hand and finger positions are held for varying lengths of time and can be combined with breath awareness, meditation or even with the physical *asanas*. *Mudras* can be practiced at any time and work via the energy channels in the hands and fingers to connect with the energy centres of the body. The effects of the *mudras*s can be intensified when combined with breath work and with focused thoughts or affirmations. There are a whole range of *mudras*, though for the purposes of bringing balance to the chakras, those which have more resonance with each particular chakra and with the element or tattwa associated with that chakra shall be selected.

In *mantra*, sounds, or Sanskrit words or phrases are sang or chanted repeatedly. Sanskrit is the ancient language of India, through which the wisdom and philosophy of the ancient texts such as the *Upanishads*, the *Bhagavad Gita* and the *Sutras* of *Patanjali* are expressed. The repetition of *mantra* is thought not only to help balance the subtle energy of the body, through the effects of the vibration of sound, but also to create a resonance with aspects of divine energy. The majority of the *mantras* are thought to have been revealed to ancient seekers of knowledge through their deep and on-going practice of meditation and the *mantras* are considered to be aspects of pure, divine consciousness, undisturbed by thought. *Mantras* can be combined with *mudra*, as well as *asana* and can form the basis for meditation, or be used to begin or end meditation or *asana* practice. For our purposes, the seed *mantras* or basic sound vibrations which correspond to the energy of each chakra shall be chosen for practice. These seed *mantras* serve to open or awaken the energy of the chakra by resonating with the particular vibration of that chakra.

With the practice of meditation we begin to harness the power of our minds by first learning to observe the mind, allowing us to detach from our thoughts rather than being controlled by them. In the ancient texts on yoga, the *Sutras* of *Patanjali*, *yoga* is defined as the cessation of the thought patterns or waves of thought within the mind. When we begin the regular practice of meditation, the mind can become less busy, less disturbed by the ripples of thought which pass through and we can perhaps experience an essence of the stillness and calm to which *Patanjali* alludes. For our purposes, the focus of meditation in each of the chakra chapters will be on the qualities associated with each chakra and on tuning into and cleansing its energy.

We can also harness the power of our mind by consciously repeating focused, positive thoughts or affirmations, chosen to awaken the particular qualities of the chakra we are focusing on. Affirmations help us to consciously direct our awareness and keep us moving towards the highest and most positive qualities of the associated chakra. For our purposes simplicity is key, so the affirmation, *mudra* and *mantra* chosen for each particular chakra will be short, sweet and effective.

With the practice of meditation we develop more choice and discernment into whether, or in what way, we act upon our thoughts in day to day life. Meditation on the chakras allows us to begin to awaken the energy of the chakra and so help us to refine and evolve our thought processes and ultimately our consciousness.

5

Further Guidance from the *Yamas* and *Niyamas*

To guide not only how we may approach the practices of yoga but also how we live and function in our lives, yoga also offers a set of inter-related principles and self-restraints. They are known as the *yamas* and *niyamas* and were outlined by *Patanjali* to bring the yogic path into every aspect of our existence.

Yamas are restraints or abstinences which help us to remain disciplined in our practice and bring more control over how we live. They help us to bring the underlying philosophy of yoga to our day to day life. They are as follows:

Non-violence (*Ahimsa*): Applying not only to the physical treatment of our own bodies and how we relate to others on the planet but also to our thoughts and attitudes to ourselves and others. This is often why a simple vegetarian diet is preferred in yoga, abstaining from harming animals as well as bringing lightness to the body. For our yoga practice, ahimsa reminds us to take care not to overstretch the body or push ourselves too far.

Truthfulness (*Satya*): Being true to ourselves, accepting our limitations and living with integrity, where our beliefs, words and behaviour are in harmony. In relation to our practice, we can also use *Satya* to ensure we work within, not beyond our abilities and to be honest with ourselves about our motivations, our intentions and our dedication to ourselves through yoga practice.

Non-stealing (*Asteya*): Living within our means and not taking what does not belong to us, referring not only to physical things, but also to credit or praise and to the time, energy or support of others. We can relate *Asteya* to balancing the level of our practice with our energy levels, ensuring we do not push too hard when energy is low or allow laziness and lethargy to develop by not taking the time to practice.

Continence (*Brahmacharya*): The principle of moderation, where we avoid becoming controlled by our desire for pleasure through sensations from sex, drugs, alcohol, food, or indeed any of the vast array of stimuli we are presented with in modern life. This does not mean avoidance of pleasure as such, rather that we exercise some discipline to safeguard against the denial and avoidance of underlying emotions through escapism or addiction. It also serves to guide us to remain steady with our practice rather than over-doing things, then finding ourselves with little energy or motivation to continue.

Non-possessiveness (*Aparigraha*): The exercise of restraint in our need for physical possessions or attributes and the recognition that our worth is not determined by what we own or what we look like, but by who we are and how we conduct ourselves within our life and relationships. With this, we remain mindful of the ultimate purpose of practice, to connect with the higher, spiritual self.

Niyamas are principles to observe in day to day life and again allow us to make the practice of yoga something which becomes part of who we are and how we live. They are as follows:

Purity (*Saucha*): The practices of yoga and meditation themselves work on helping us cleanse the body and the mind allowing us to clear toxins from the body and negativity from the mind. Observance of purity reminds us to keep focused, to have an uncluttered environment, a simple approach to how we live and how we think, creating a clearer path to progress through life.

Contentment (*Santosha*): Reminding us to be happy with what we have, to practice acceptance and gratitude and to acknowledge each moment as it arises without judgement. It is not about escapism or retreating from life through avoidance of reality but rather cultivation of contentment for all that we experience. When we practice yoga with contentment, we avoid judging ourselves harshly and are more able to stay completely in the present moment, helping our practice become not only more effective, but also more joyful.

Austerity (*Tapas*): Urges us to be disciplined and to commit to our practice. *Tapas* refers to burning away the obstacles to strength of body and clarity of mind through the practices of yoga, allowing our energy to become clear and our inner light to shine through. It encourages us to commit to practice and ultimately to trust that regular practice brings its own rewards through better health, happiness and spiritual growth.

Study (*Swadhyaya*): Encourages us to engage with life, to enhance our knowledge and creativity and to study. This study is not only to enhance our theoretical knowledge but also to study ourselves, our relationships and behaviour and the workings of our mind. When we practice yoga we can observe ourselves and our thoughts, without judgment and begin to notice and let go of the habits which hinder us from being truly present.

Attentitiveness to the Divine (*Ishvara Pranidhana*): Awareness of divine or universal consciousness rather than focusing on the individual ego and its needs. This allows us to cultivate a sense of that which is beyond our individual mind and understanding and bring a sense of spiritual purpose to the day to day activities of life. In adversity, it encourages us to remain focused on our development and accept that we can learn from all we experience. It brings a more spiritual aspect to our yoga practice and helps us awaken the higher consciousness within.

Patanjali saw the practice of yoga as a journey, through which we can ultimately come to realise our true self and connect with the universal consciousness. The *Yamas* and *Niyamas* are there to guide us in this journey. They allow our yoga practice to be enhanced and also bring the practice into everyday life rather than limiting it to an allotted time on the yoga mat.

For many of us, the idea of self-realisation can seem a distant and esoteric concept, so a practice which is systematic and accessible will allow us to proceed with simplicity and ease.

Observance of the *Yamas* and *Niyamas* and the focused application of *asana*, *pranayama*, *mantra*, *mudra*, meditation and positive affirmation to each of the energy centres of the body creates a path to awakening, re-vitalising and purifying the body and creating a calm and balanced mind. When we begin to experience the benefits of improved health, a more peaceful mind and a greater harmony in our relationship with ourselves, others and how we approach and experience our lives, we can experience yoga as the spiritual journey *Patanjali* described so long ago.

6

How to Use the Book

In the following chapters we shall work through each of the chakras, beginning from the base, or root chakra and ascending to the crown.

Each chapter begins with an outline of the chakra, describing the qualities associated with the energy of the chakra and the related physical and behavioural attributes.

We then go on to the 'how to' section which will give the breathing exercises, physical postures, *mudra*, *mantra*, and meditation to begin to awaken and re-balance the energy of the chakra. We end with some ideas of activities we can do in day to day life to strengthen the energy.

The final four chapters outline practices which help balance all of the chakras. The first, in Chapter 15 is a short exercise which can be done at any time and describes simple breathing exercises linked to each chakra. Chapter 16 describes the energising practice of sun salutations which are ideally done early morning, though can be used at any time whenever energy is low, helping to re-vitalise body and mind and bring balance to the whole energy system. Following this in Chapter 17 is a restorative practice which can be used in the evening, or pre-bedtime, or indeed at any time when the need for a quieter and more restful practice is felt. In Chapter 18 a short meditation on all of the chakras is described, combining the associated *mudra* and *mantra*.

It is advised to work on each of the chakras from root to crown. Each chapter is its own self-contained practice and it is recommended that a commitment is made to practice regularly. Ideally a daily practice will be most effective, though if this is impractical, then every two to three days or even a weekly practice will bring benefits. The morning and evening practices outlined in Chapters 16 and 17 can also be used on a daily basis, or if impractical, every two to three days or again on a weekly basis. They will give a 'fine-tuning' to the whole energy system, particularly useful during intervals between each individual chakra practice. The same principles apply to the short practices in Chapters 15 and 18 which are also an effective way to end any of the individual chakra practices.

Make space to practice by clearing a space for your yoga mat in your home and making sure you are where possible, undisturbed. Make a commitment to yourself, have patience and enjoy.

Before beginning, please take medical consultation if there are any medical conditions or you are on medication. For beginners to yoga, it is advised that where possible you attend a beginner's class for some time to become familiar with the *asanas* and breath-work so as to gain more benefit from the book. Please also note the contra-indications outlined for some of the postures and breathing exercises. Only practice *asanas* you are comfortable with and work up to the more challenging *asanas* slowly. Proceed with care, listening to the needs of the body, not pushing beyond what feels right for you, on that particular day of practice. Our energy levels can fluctuate throughout the day and from one day or week to another, so be mindful of how you feel before beginning. It is possible to do only one or two of the *asanas* from each chapter, then proceed with breathing and meditation where you are unable, through lack of time or energy to do all. If so, please choose with care and avoid going into a more challenging *asana* without preliminary warming up of the body.

For that purpose, a short routine is outlined in Chapter 7 and it is advised to practice this before proceeding with each chakra chapter, particularly if you are relatively new to yoga or are unable to attend a class. The exercises wake up the energy body, ensure the joints of the body are warmed up, the internal organs energised and the muscles lengthened before *asana* begins. Indeed, when time is short, just doing the warm-up on its own, rather than no practice at all will benefit the body. The warm up is short, deceptively simple, yet highly effective. It is an ideal morning exercise, allowing the body to awaken and energy to flow. On its own, or followed by the sun salutations, the breathing exercises or the short meditation in chapters sixteen, fifteen and eighteen, it is an excellent way to start the day.

7

Warm and Awaken the Body

Begin by standing with feet hip-width apart and parallel and the top of the head rising to the sky, tail-bone releasing to the earth and the soles of the feet gently pressing into the floor beneath, with the arches of the feet lifted. Take awareness to the breath and feel your rib-cage, heart and chest open and expand with each inhale and soften and release with each exhale. Soften the eyes and allow the mind to quieten as you become more tuned in to the gentle rhythm of your breath, and make an intention to warm, open and awaken your body.

Neck and Head

With the collar-bones wide and shoulders drawn down from the ears, place the hands on the hips and begin circling the head, keeping the back of the neck long. Visualise the nose is drawing a circle in front of the face and the skull is circling around on top of the spine. Pause and circle in the other direction.

With the neck long and chin parallel to the floor, drop the chin to the base of the throat and allow the back of the neck to lengthen. Stay for five long, even breaths, releasing tension from the large muscles of the neck. Take the head back to centre and allow the side of the head to drop towards the right shoulder, allowing the left side of the neck to lengthen, ensuring the chin remains centred to the chest. Take five long, even breaths. Repeat on the left, then circle the head two or three times in each direction.

Take the fingertips of both hands and tap all over the

scalp for 1–2 minutes until the scalp tingles with energy. Squeeze and massage the outer part of the ears between the thumbs and first fingers, beginning at the tops of the ears and working down to the ear-lobes. Repeat several times until the ears feel warm and energised.

Take the third fingers to the space between the eyebrows and draw them out to the sides of the head, across the eyebrows. Work upwards through the forehead, opening and widening the forehead and brow.

Take the first and middle fingers to the temples of the head and make gentle circular movements outwards towards the sides of the head until the temples feel relaxed. Bring the hands to a soft fist, take the knuckles under the cheek-bones at the sides of the nose and work outwards to the ears, with small circular movements. Repeat a few times until the cheeks feel energised, then finish by pinching along the jaw-line several times, from the chin to the ears with the thumbs and first fingers, until the jaw feels firm.

Take the fingers to the top of the neck and make small circular movements, working down the muscles on either side of the spine, down to the base of the neck. Repeat several times until the neck muscles feel relaxed.

Shoulders

Take the left hand to the right shoulder at the base of the neck and squeeze the muscles along the back of the shoulder, working outwards to the arm. Repeat several times then do the same with the left shoulder.

Draw the shoulders to the ears as you inhale, then draw them back, slide the shoulder-blades towards each other and sighing the breath out through the mouth, drop them down. Repeat several times, allowing tension to be released.

Circle the shoulders back to the wall behind as you breathe in, opening and widening the collarbones and release down as you exhale. Make the circling movements smooth and even, feeling the breath in the upper chest and back and allowing the whole shoulder, collar-bone and chest area to release tightness and tension.

Wrists and Hands

Take the base of the right thumb between the thumb and finger of the left hand and gently twist back and forth as you work to the tip of the thumb. Repeat with the fingers, then with the left hand, until you feel energy flowing through the fingers and thumbs. Clap the palms together several times, then clap the backs of the hands together, then the thumb sides and pinkie sides of the hands. Shake the hands and feel energy flow through the hands to the tips of the fingers

Circle the hands, drawing the fingers in as if to touch the inside of the wrists, then out again 8 – 10 times, then repeat in the other direction. Feel the wrist joints warming up and energy flowing into the hands and fingers.

Take the arms out in front of you at shoulder level. Take the thumbs into the palms and wrap the fingers around the thumbs. Circle the hands five times clockwise, five times anti-clockwise releasing the wrist joints.

Squeeze the fingers around the thumbs as you breathe in. Exhale through the mouth, blowing the breath out as though blowing lots of candles out on a cake and at the same time fully extend the fingers and thumbs, spreading them wide. Repeat five times. Finish by vigorously rubbing the palms together.

Arms, Torso and Hips

Take the left hand into a soft fist and begin gently pounding the muscle of the right arm, working from the top of the outer arm to the wrist, then turn and work upwards along the inner arm. Repeat several times until you feel energy flowing through the arm, then work on the left arm with the right fist.

Inhale and raise both arms up in front of the body, stretching the arms to the sky, palms facing forwards. Feel the front of the torso open and lengthen. Exhale and float the arms down in front of the body, then back by the sides. Repeat five times.

Inhale and raise the arms out to the sides and lift and stretch to the sky with the palms facing outwards. Feel the sides of the torso open and lengthen from the waist to the fingertips. Exhale and float the arms back down. Repeat five times.

Take a nice big breath into the chest and heart and with the fingers, gently tap all over the chest as you hold the inhale, working from the centre of the chest outwards. Exhale and let go. Repeat several times then do the same exercise, working from the centre of the rib-cage out to the sides of the body, until you feel the chest and rib-cage filled with energy.

Take the palms of the hands together, thumbs resting in the centre of the upper chest and rub the thumb sides of the hands up and down over the upper chest and heart area for 1 – 2 minutes, then breathe slowly and evenly tuning in to the energy of the heart.

Take the palm of the hand onto the belly and begin to make circular clockwise movements over the whole of the abdomen until you feel the area warming, the internal organs wakening and the abdomen energised.

Take the hands onto the hips and begin to circle the hips clockwise, making the circling movement larger as the hips open. Feel the hips stretch to the side, the front and out into the lower back. Circle around ten times and repeat in the other direction.

Raise the right leg with the knee bent, level with the hip and take the right hand onto the knee. Circle the knee five times outwards from the body, keeping the spine straight and feel the hip opening. Repeat five times, circling the knee inwards, then do the same with the left leg until both hips feel open.

Back and Legs

Take both hands to a soft fist at the top of the right leg and begin to gently pound down the outside muscle of the right leg, then upwards on the inside. Repeat several times then do the same with the left leg until you feel energy flowing through the legs.

Breathe in and stretch the arms out to the sides and over the head. Interlace the fingers and stretch the palms of the hands to the sky, making the body tall and the spine long. Exhale and bend the knees, coming into a squat, with the palms down on the floor. Straighten the legs and allow the body to hang down in a loose forward bend, top of the head releasing to the floor. At the end of your exhale, draw the belly to the back of the body, gently press the heels down into the mat and feel the buttock bones lengthen to the sky.

As you inhale, begin to uncurl the spine, keeping the belly drawn to the back of the body and awareness on each of the vertebrae of your spine gently unrolling, head coming up last. Repeat five times and on the fifth, allow the body to hang down and stay for five even breaths. With each exhale, draw the belly to the back of the body, press the feet down and lengthen the base of the spine and buttock bones to the sky, the top of the head to the earth. Slowly uncurl on an inhale and stay focused on the breath while you feel the benefits of the practice and the length created in the spine and hamstring muscles.

Take the hands into soft fists and rub the soft part of the back of your waist and lower back, warming and energising the kidneys and lower back.

Ankles and Feet

Sit down, stretch the legs out in front of you and circle the feet, working to open the ankle joints. Repeat 5 or 6 times in each direction.

Stretch the feet out, pointing the toes, opening the front of the foot and ankle as you breathe in. Exhaling, stretch the soles of the feet and the heels away from you and the toes towards you, feeling the backs of the legs lengthen. Repeat five or six times.

Curl the toes tightly as you breathe in and stretch them out and away from each other as you breathe out. Repeat five or six times.

Finally take the base of the big toe of the right foot between the finger and thumb of the left and twist back and forth to the top of the toe. Repeat with all toes until you feel energy flowing in the toes, then take the tips of the fingers and thumb of the left hand together into a point and tap all over the sole of the right foot until it too feels energised. Repeat with the left foot. Finish by gently shaking the legs and feet.

Come to stand, take a few deep and even breaths, ready to begin your chakra practice, sun salutation, breathing or meditation or simply ready and energised for your day ahead.

8

Awakening *Mooladhara* Chakra

Mooladhara chakra lies at the base of the body and is symbolized by a red lotus with four petals. In the centre is a yellow square which represents the earth element, known in Sanskrit as *prithvi tattwa*. The *bija* or seed *mantra* for *Mooladhara* chakra is Lam, its colour is red and apana energy, the energy of elimination is governed here, enabling us to expel waste from the body and let go of the things we no longer need.

Known as the base chakra, *Mooladhara* translates from Sanskrit as 'root support' and forms the foundation of the energy system. Spinning at a slower rate than the other chakras, it links us to earth energy and to the material, physical world. When *Mooladhara* is awakened we are able to nurture our physical body and take care of our environment. We feel secure and stable and can proceed through life with a quiet confidence, certain of the firm base from which we can grow. A balanced *Mooladhara* draws earth energy up through the legs where it can be processed and can also send excess energy in the body back to the earth, literally keeping us grounded. It is here that the three main energy channels, *Sushumna*, *Ida* and *Pingala* are merged and where our full potential, known in yoga as *kundalini* energy, is housed. From *Mooladhara*, *Ida* and *Pingala* separate and travel upwards, to merge once more at *Ajna* chakra. As we awaken and balance the chakras, the dormant *kundalini* begins to rise upwards through *Sushumna* and when fully awakened it reaches the crown chakra *Sahasrara*, where our individual consciousness merges with that of the universe. *Mooladhara* is the firm basis we need to begin the journey from the physical to the spiritual plane of existence.

Physically, it is located between behind the pubic bone at the front of the body and connects to the tailbone at the base of the spine. Its centre is the perineum in males and the cervix in females. It is associated with the skeletal system, the teeth, hips, legs and feet, and the bowels. It is also linked to the nose and our sense of smell, the most primitive of the senses, which is so well developed in the animal world and so essential to their survival. Our survival mechanism, the fight or flight response, regulated by the adrenal glands is also influenced by *Mooladhara* energy. It is very much about our instinctive nature, our ability to be completely present within our body and aware of our surrounding environment.

Qualities Associated with a Balanced Base Chakra

When *Mooladhara* is balanced we feel grounded and protected. We have good energy levels, inner strength and satisfaction with our lot in life. Positive relationships with others, particularly family members are common, as we are more likely to have experienced a positive and secure early childhood. With good early nurturing we feel more able to nurture ourselves and take care of our physical body, contributing to a sense of confidence and independence. Our 'base' on earth is secure, reflecting the balanced base of the energy system, so we are likely to experience satisfaction with our job and our home. We are more likely to be patient and to adopt an optimistic approach to life and its challenges.

Problems Associated with an Imbalanced Base Chakra

When the energy of *Mooladhara* is imbalanced it may be reflected in dis-ease or dysfunction in the teeth or jaw, the lower back, hips, knees and feet. It is also linked to problems in the lower intestine such as constipation, colitis or irritable bowel syndrome and to eating disorders and obesity. Low energy and chronic fatigue may also arise when *Mooladhara* is imbalanced. We may feel dis-connected to our body, unable to take care of ourselves physically and experience a feeling of un-groundedness, a lack of direction in life and a sense of disorientation and indecision.

Greed, workaholism, and being overly focused on material possessions also reflect an imbalance here, where we feel the urge to collect and hoard rather than let go, and we view the world only as a resource to be consumed and disposed of without due care and respect. Our focus on money and material possessions to the detriment of the environment reflects on a societal level, the imbalance in *Mooladhara* energy.

How to Awaken *Mooladhara* Chakra

Breathing

Sit in any comfortable seated posture with the spine lengthened and breathe in deeply through both nostrils, drawing the breath down into the lower abdomen, the pelvis and the lower back. As you breathe, feel that you are drinking the breath in, filling the pelvis and drawing the breath down to the sitting bones and tail-bone. Feel the base of the body broaden and expand on your inhale. As you exhale gently draw the pelvic floor muscles up into the body and the lower abdomen back towards the spine. Take 15 to 20 slow, balanced breaths.

Moola Bandha (root lock)

In a comfortable, seated posture, relax and draw awareness to the base of the body. Breathe in, contract and lift the pelvic floor upwards (the perineum area in males, the neck of the womb in females). Hold for a few seconds, exhale and relax. Repeat up to ten times. Initially the whole of the base of the body may lift upwards, including the anus and the urinary tract, but over time greater awareness develops and you will find it easier to isolate *moola bandha*.

Benefits: Strengthens and tones the internal muscles and improves the functioning of the urinary, reproductive and intestinal systems.

Physical Exercises

Tadasana (Mountain Pose)

- Engage a gentle moola bandha, by lightly drawing the pelvic floor muscles upwards into the body. Stand with the feet together and allow the lower abdominal muscles to draw back slightly, towards the spine.
- Allow the pelvis to be neutral, neither tipping forwards, nor swaying backwards and allow the base of the spine to lengthen downwards towards the heels.
- Feel the soles of your feet open and connected to the earth beneath. Gently press the soles of the feet into the floor and as you do so, be aware of the legs, the spine and the crown of your head lengthening upwards towards the sky.
- Allow the arms to extend downwards along the sides of the body and gently open and lift the chest, feeling the shoulders relaxing and the collar-bones widening. Breathe evenly and smoothly, allowing the rib-cage to expand as you inhale, keeping the abdominals engaged

and gently drawn to the back of the body. Visualise yourself strong, stable and connected to earth, like a mountain.

Benefits: Improved posture, strengthened legs, straightened spine.

***Vriksasana* (tree pose)**

- From *Tadasana*, allow the weight of your body to flow down into your right foot.
- Press the foot down and feel the body grow taller. With your eyes cast downwards, bend the left knee, open the left hip and the knee outwards and place the sole of the left foot against the inner right ankle, calf, knee or thigh, depending on comfort and flexibility.
- Take the hands to prayer posture, with the thumbs resting in the heart centre and breathe evenly. Inhaling, raise the hands, still in prayer, above the head.
- Lengthen the body from the sides of the waist through the arms, to the tips of the fingers, like the branches of a tree rising to the sky.
- Stay for five to ten slow, even breaths, aware of inner balance and strength and feel the standing leg foot rooted to the earth.
- Slowly lower your hands back to the heart and the foot to the floor. Pause and repeat on the other side, then return to *Tadasana*.

Benefits: Improved stability and balance, lengthened spine, improved flexibility in the knees and hips, and helps improve concentration.

***Adho Mukha Svanasana* (downward-facing dog pose)**

- From *Tadasana*, kneel down, tuck the toes under and sit on the heels. Bend forwards from the hips, arms lengthened, shoulder width apart and place the hands down on the floor.
- Stretch the arms as far forwards as is comfortable, spread the fingers, with the index and middle fingers facing forwards. Press the palms of the hands and the pads of the fingers and thumbs into the floor.
- Widen across the collar bones and shoulders and draw the shoulder blades down the back. As you exhale, draw the belly back towards the spine and unfold the legs.
- Lift the hips and the tailbone up to the ceiling and back to the wall behind, creating a long spine and lengthened torso and allow the heels to release towards the floor, lengthening the hamstrings.
- Stay for 10 to 15 slow, even breaths, drawing the breath down to the tailbone. Bend your knees, come back to kneel then as you inhale, return to *Tadasana*.

Benefits: Strengthens the back, shoulders and arms, tones the legs and lengthens the hamstrings. It also has a calming effect on the mind.

***Virabhadrasana 2* (warrior 2 pose)**

- From *Tadasana*, step the feet three to four feet apart.
- Turn the right foot out, parallel to the sides of the mat and the left foot, slightly inwards, with the right heel in line with the arch of the left foot.
- Exhale and draw the pelvic floor muscles up into the body and the abdominals back towards the spine. Inhale, lengthen the spine and draw the top of your head to the ceiling.
- Bend the right knee, ensuring the knee sits above the ankle and is line with the centre toe, allowing the right inner thigh to lengthen.
- Raise both arms to shoulder level, palms facing down and lengthen the arms away from each other, widening the collar-bones and the backs of the shoulders and stretching the fingers to opposite walls.
- Keep the top of the head lifting to the ceiling, in line with the base of the spine and draw the chin in to lengthen the back of the neck. Turn the head to look along the right arm, keeping the shoulders relaxed.
- Press the soles of your feet into the floor and feel the legs and spine lengthening. Hug your thigh muscles to your thigh bones and keep the back leg straight with the outer edge of the back heel pressed down to the floor. Hold for five to 10 smooth even breaths, feeling the strength and openness of the pose.
- Exhale, drop the arms to the sides, then repeat on the left side and return to *Tadasana*.

Benefits: Strengthens the lower back and legs, tones the arms and opens the shoulders.

Prasarita Paddottonasana **(wide leg forward stretch)**

- From *Tadasana*, take the feet three to four feet apart, with feet parallel. Place the hands on the hips, lift the pelvis and hinge forwards from the hips into flat back with the spine lengthened and the abdominals drawn towards the back of the body.
- Lengthen your tail-bone and sitting bones to the wall behind, exhale, lift the lower abdomen towards the spine and lower the crown of the head to the floor, placing the hands between the feet, palms down and fingers facing forwards (bend the knees if the fingers or hands do not come to the floor).
- Bend the elbows to the wall behind, keeping them in line with the shoulders and above the wrists.
- Release the crown of the head to the floor, lift the tail-bone and sitting bones to the ceiling and rotate the backs of your thighs away from each other. Firm the outer edges of the feet into the floor and feel the legs and spine lengthening. Stay for five to ten deep, even breaths, drawing the breath to the tailbone. On an inhale, engage the abdominals, lengthen and raise the spine back to 'flat back', then back to vertical and step the feet together, returning to *Tadasana*.

Benefits: Strengthens the legs, lengthens the spine, opens the hips and calms the mind. (Only bend to 'flat back' position, if there are serious back problems or high blood pressure).

Relaxation

Rest in *Shavasana*, relaxation pose, by lengthening and unrolling your spine down onto the floor. Lengthen the legs out, allow space between the heels, with pinkie toe sides of the feet releasing to the floor and thigh bones releasing away from each other. Draw the shoulder-blades towards each other, widen and open the chest and collar-bones and allow the upper arms to externally rotate, so the backs of the hands can lie on the floor with the palms facing upwards. Stay for five minutes, focusing on the gentle rise and fall of your breath, allowing your body to experience the benefits of your practice.

Meditation

In cross- legged position, allow the hips to relax and feel the sitting bones rooted down into the earth with the spine lengthened. Come to *Prithvi mudra*, the earth *mudra*, by connecting the tips of the thumbs and third fingers together, with the other fingers extended, palms open, resting on the knees and facing down to the earth. Allow your breath to deepen on your inhale and feel you are drawing the breath down into the tail-bone, hips and lower back. Soften the lower abdomen with each exhale. Visualise the colour red and see it as a clear rotating circle of ruby light, slowly spinning (horizontally and clock-wise) at the base or seat of the body. Focus on your connection with the earth and feel that you are drawing positive energy up from the earth as you inhale and releasing and connecting to the earth as you exhale. Stay with the practice for several minutes and each time your awareness wanders off with your thoughts, gently draw it back to the breath. With practice build up to ten minutes or more.

Silently affirm, 'I am safe and secure. I trust the earth to nourish and protect me.' Chant the *mantra* LAM (pronounced l-a-u-m) 10 times on an exhale, slowly inhaling between each chant. Focus on sensing the vibration of the sound within you and on your base chakra becoming balanced and clear.

Sit quietly for a few minutes noticing any after effects of your practice.

Activities to Strengthen *Mooladhara* Energy

Take time to clean your home and de-clutter regularly. Ensure your living environment is as pleasant and comfortable as it can be; a space where you feel secure and relaxed.

Look after your feet, an often neglected part of the body. Make a foot soak, pedicure and foot massage part of your body care routine. Ensure shoes are well-fitting and comfortable.

Walk barefoot whenever you can, taking time to connect with the feel of grass, sand or earth, beneath your feet.

Make time to be with your family, appreciative of your relationship with them and of the role of your ancestors before.

Garden or tend to an allotment or to house-plants. Feed the birds, look after animals, become involved in an environmental group. Connect with and look after, the earth.

Although living in an age of materialism, resist the urge to buy things for no reason and look after the possessions you have. Refuse to be part of the 'consume and throw away' culture. Recycle and re-use.

Enjoy the sense of smell, take time to smell the flowers, the aromas of the natural world and use aromatherapy oils to keep your home naturally scented, with clean, clear air.

9

Awakening *Swadhisthana* Chakra

Situated in the lower abdomen, is *Swadhisthana* chakra, the sacral chakra. This chakra is symbolised as a crimson lotus with six petals. In the centre is a white crescent moon representing apas tattwa, the water element. The seed or *bija mantra* associated with *Swadisthana* is Vam, its colour is orange and like *Mooladhara* chakra, apana energy is also governed here, the energy of release and letting go.

Connected to pleasure, sensuality and creativity, *Swadhisthana* means sweet or sacred place and holds our unconscious desires and fantasies. When its energy becomes active it can reflect our more primitive desires for pleasure and enjoyment, with the risk of addictive behaviours developing. By purifying and balancing this centre however, we can transcend these desires and the energy can be expressed in creative activities. It is linked to our sexuality and sexual interactions so it is also about how we relate to others and how we can accept ourselves as sexual beings, without shame and guilt. Reflecting the water element, *Swadisthana* is concerned with fluidity and flexibility, our ability to adapt and go with the flow, both in our relationships and in the challenges we encounter in life.

At a physical level, *Swadhisthana* is associated with liquid in the body, such as blood and urine, and with the sexual organs, bladder, hips, pelvis, and lower back. It also connects with the tongue and the sense of taste. It is linked to the reproductive organs and glands, involved in our sexual development, fertility and ability to procreate. Like

Mooladhara, *Swadhisthana* also has a link to the adrenal glands, as its energy is also about our survival in the world, our ability to adapt to perceived threat and overcome challenges. Its energy can help us overcome our fear, forge positive, healthy relationships with ourselves and other people and enable us to recognise and embrace the sweet things in life.

Qualities Associated with a Balanced Second Chakra

When the chakra is balanced the individual is likely to have good awareness of their personal boundaries and limits and can accept themselves as they are. As a result, they are able to develop nurturing relationships with others, see their sexual desires as a positive aspect of their life and feel deserving of love and respect. They can be generous, are comfortable in their own skin and are able to enjoy life's pleasures. They are also non-judgemental, accepting other people as they are. Able to defend themself, they can 'stand their ground' and show resilience when faced with difficulty, able to 'bounce back' from troubled times. They are often creative, able to express themselves artistically and can adopt a creative approach to life, showing an ability to adapt to circumstance, reflecting the fluidity of *Swadhisthana* energy.

Problems Associated with an Imbalanced Second Chakra

With an imbalance there may be problems around control, with addictive behaviours developing, when desires are acted upon without limit and the sensual pleasures of life assume primary importance. There may also be issues around control in relationships, with fears of rejection and abandonment, so relationships are often unstable and full of drama and emotion. A sense of restlessness and anxiety may be present, with obsessive and compulsive behaviour developing to mask inner fears. Rigidity, absence of creativity and an inability to adapt to change may be present, preventing the individual from moving through life, instead feeling stuck and frustrated with their lot. On a physical level, imbalance may be reflected with lower back problems, sexual, fertility and gynaecological problems, or problems with the kidneys and bladder.

How to Awaken *Swadhisthana* Chakra

Breathing

Crescent Moon Breath

Sit in a comfortable posture with the sitting bones rooted down into the floor beneath, spine lengthened and the top of the head rising to an imagined night sky above. Gently draw the breath down into the lower abdomen and lower back. Visualise a crescent moon lying on its' side from hip-bone to hip-bone, across the pelvis. As you breathe in, imagine you are tracing the outline of the top part of the crescent moon, from right hip to left hip and as you breathe out, trace the lower and longer outline of the crescent moon, from left hip to right hip. Your exhalation will be slightly longer than your inhalation. Keep the breath slow, even and steady and allow the body to become more relaxed and the mind become quieter. Stay for two to three minutes, then let go of the visualisation and take a few even, balanced breaths down into the lower abdomen.

Physical Exercises

Padahastasana (hand to foot pose)

- Stand in *Tadasana*, with the spine lengthened and take the feet hip width apart and parallel, arms by the sides.
- As you exhale draw the lower abdomen to the back of the body and bend forwards from the hips until the back is parallel to the floor, allowing the arms to hang down.
- On your next exhale, bend forwards further, allowing the spine to lengthen and the top of the head to release to the floor with the sitting bones and tailbone rising to the ceiling.
- Take the hands to the sides of the feet (or to the sides of the ankles or shins) and draw the face in towards the legs, keeping the back of the neck lengthened (with practice, the palms rest beside the feet).
- With each exhale, draw the lower abdomen to the back of the body and with each inhale breathe into the back of the rib-cage and lengthen the spine. Soften, or slightly bend, the backs of the knees to prevent over-stretching the hamstring muscles.
- Stay for three to five slow breaths, then lengthen the spine, engage the abdominal muscles and take the back parallel to the floor once more, before returning to *Tadasana*.

Benefits: Massages and tones the organs in the lower abdomen, improves flexibility in the hamstrings and lengthens the spine (only bend to 'flat back' where the spine is parallel to the floor if there are serious back complaints or high blood pressure).

Ashwa Sanchalanasana **(equestrian pose)**

- From *Tadasana*, bend forwards from the hips, bend the knees, and take the fingertips onto the floor at the side of each foot. Step the left leg back and keep the right knee above the ankle.
- Lightly press the fingers onto the floor, open and lift the chest, draw the shoulder-blades down the back and keep the chin parallel to the floor with the crown of the head lifting to the ceiling.
- Lengthen the left hip to the heel and the heel to the wall behind, feeling the left hip and lower abdomen gently stretching and opening.
- Breathe slowly for four to eight breaths, then step the left foot forwards besides the right foot and repeat on the other side.

Benefits: Opens the lower abdomen, strengthens the hips, legs, knees and feet. (Avoid if there are serious knee or ankle problems).

***Gatyatmak Paschimottanasana* (dynamic back stretch pose)**

- Sit on the floor in *Dandasana* with the sitting bones rooted down and the spine lengthened.
- Lengthen the legs out, with the soles of the feet pressed against an imaginary wall and legs and feet together.
- Breathe in and raise both arms upwards, then keeping the arms above the head, engage the abdominal muscles and unroll the back of the body onto the floor behind, with the arms lengthened to the wall behind. Pause briefly and exhale.
- As you breathe in, engage the abdominal muscles and lift the trunk back to a seated position, with the spine lengthened and the arms stretched above the head (if this proves difficult, lower the arms and press the hands into the floor to help lift the trunk, until the abdominals are stronger).
- Exhale, draw the abdomen to the spine and bend forward from the hips, with the arms by the sides of the legs. Pause briefly, holding the breath.
- Inhale and come back to the seated posture with arms above the head.
- This is one round. Repeat up to five times and with practice, build up to ten rounds.

Benefits: Tones and massages all of the pelvic and abdominal organs as well as strengthening the abdomen, back and spine. (Avoid if there are any back problems, heart disease or high blood pressure).

Chakki Chalanasana (grinding pose)

- Sit in *Dandasana* posture, with the spine lengthened, the sitting bones gently pressing into the floor, top of the head lengthening to the ceiling and the legs outstretched.
- Take the legs two to three feet apart, with the soles of the feet pressed against an imaginary wall.
- Interlace the fingers and stretch both arms out in front of the chest, keeping the arms straight throughout the practice, without bending the elbows.

- Turn the trunk and the arms to face the left leg and exhaling, bend forwards over the knee.
- Moving clockwise, take the body over the right knee, then inhaling lean back as far as is comfortable.
- Continue to rotate clockwise nine times, keeping awareness on the breath. Pause and repeat the movement nine times, turning anticlockwise over the legs.
- Focus on the waist and lower abdomen maintaining a circular movement and make the movement as expansive as you can, imagining you are stirring around the edges of a large circular pot, the hands clasping a large wooden spoon.
- Breathe out as you circle forwards; breathe in as you circle back.

Benefits: Energises the lower abdominal and pelvic organs and can help regulate the menstrual cycle. (Avoid after the first three months of pregnancy).

***Merudandasana* (spinal column pose)**

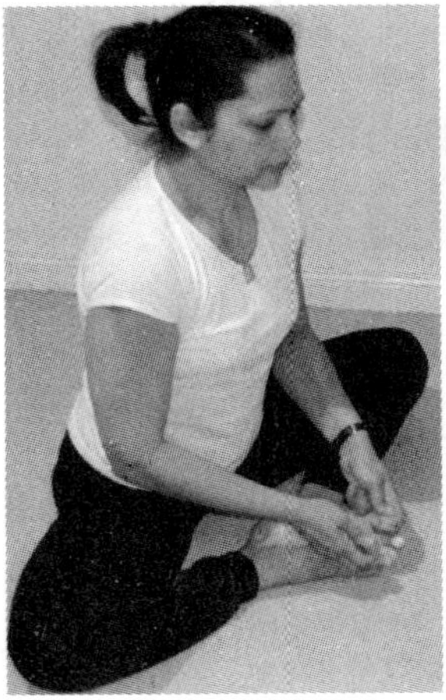

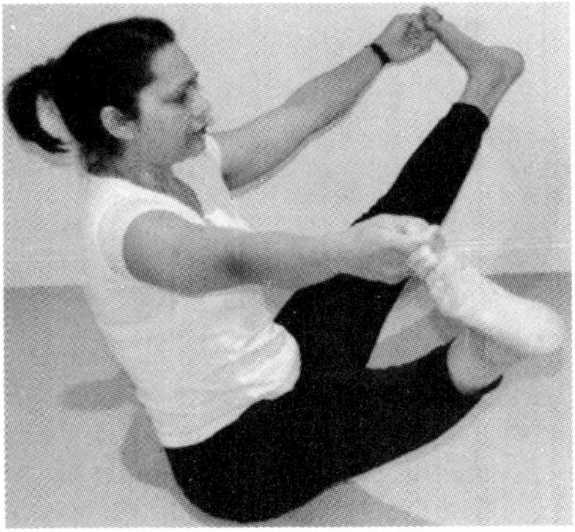

- Sit in *Dandasana*, bend the knees, open the thighs and take the soles of the feet together. Draw the heels inwards to the body and curl the first two fingers of each hand around the big toes, in bound angle or *Baddha Konasana* posture.

- Inhale, tilt backwards slightly and begin to raise the legs upwards and outwards, keeping the spine lengthened and the sitting bones pressing down. Keep the fingers around the big toes or if this proves difficult, hold the ankles.
- Lift the torso up from the hips and keep the spine lengthened, whilst maintaining its natural curve. Lift and open the inner thighs. With practice, work towards straightening the legs, without over-stretching.
- Relax the shoulders down from the ears, open the collarbones and lift the chest.
- Breathe deeply and slowly into the lower abdomen for five breaths. Bend the knees, take the soles of the feet together and return to *Baddha Konasana*. With practice, repeat the pose another two to three times.

Benefits: Strengthens the spine and legs and opens the lower back and pelvis. (Avoid if there are back problems such as slipped disc or sciatica).

***Koormasana* (tortoise pose)**

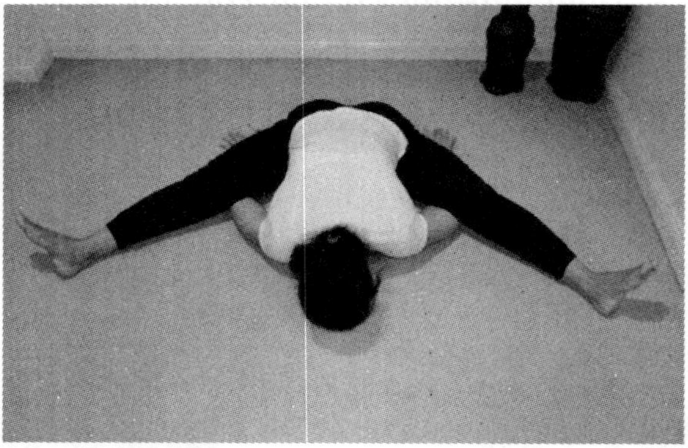

- From *Dandasana*, bend the knees and place the heels on the floor with the soles of the feet facing the wall in front.
- Bend forwards from the hips and slide the hands under the knees, palms facing down or up, whichever feels more comfortable.
- Lengthen the arms out underneath the knees and gradually draw the backs of the knees down over the arms.

- On an inhale, deepen the pose by stretching the legs and firmly pressing the heels forwards. Press the legs down on the backs of the upper arms and shoulders, drawing the torso closer to the floor.
- Open the chest and lengthen forwards and down as you continue to stretch out the arms. Stay for 5 to 10 slow, even breaths.
- With practice, the body will come further to the floor and in the final posture the chin rests on the floor.
- Slowly return to the starting position.

Benefits: Tones the pelvic and abdominal organs, lengthens the spine and hamstrings, opens the shoulders and improves circulation in the back and spine. (Avoid if there are serious back problems and approach slowly and with care if the spine is not yet flexible).

Relaxation

Rest for five minutes in *Shavasana* (as outlined in *Mooladhara* chapter) focusing on the breath and allowing the body to feel the benefits of your practice.

Meditation

In cross-legged position, allow the hips to relax and feel the sitting bones rooted down into the earth. Come to *Bhudi mudra*, the fluid *mudra*, by touching the tips of the little fingers to the thumbs, other fingers extended and palms facing upwards, with the backs of the hands resting on the knees. With the spine lengthened, gently draw the breath to the lower abdomen and focus on the space between the hips. Visualise a circle of bright orange light, gently spinning (horizontally and clockwise) in the lower abdomen. See this light become clear and bright. Focus on the element of water and the idea of fluidity and flow. Stay with the practice for several minutes and each time your awareness wanders off with your thoughts, gently draw it back to the breath. With practice build up to ten minutes or more. Silently affirm 'I am creative, I flow through life, with all my needs and desires in perfect balance with the universe'. Slowly chant VAM (pronounced v-a-u-m) ten times on an exhale, slowly breathing in between each chant. Focus on sensing vibration in the lower abdomen and the chakra energy becoming clear, shining and pure. Sit quietly for a few minutes, noticing any after-effects of your practice.

Activities to Strengthen *Swadhisthana* Energy

Bathe, swim and enjoy being in water as often as you can. Wash your hands regularly throughout the day and ensure you are drinking enough water. Enjoy the sensation of water, washing away negative energy, detoxing the body and refreshing you physically and emotionally.

Pay attention to the cycles of the moon and be aware of your energy levels when the moon is rising and when it is waning. At the time of the new and the full moon make time to meditate, with a special focus on your intentions for the month ahead.

Exercise restraint with addictive substances such as alcohol or caffeine and be aware of your cravings for substances. Spend a few days every month, or one day per week, de-toxing the body, by eating wholesome fruits, vegetables, soups and juices.

Be creative. Enrol in a class or enjoy at home, an activity where you make something from scratch through painting, pottery, sewing, knitting, woodwork etc. Do not judge your attempts, instead focus on enjoying the process.

Enjoy sensual pleasures such as touch and taste and accept yourself as a sexual, sensual being. Have a massage or enjoy massaging your skin with oil or lotion after bathing. Slow down when eating, enjoying the pleasure and taste of your meal.

Value and nurture your relationships with family and friends. Make time to see those in your life who are important to you.

Accept and express your emotions. Let go of guilt by forgiving yourself and reminding yourself of your own and others' vulnerability and essential humanness.

10

Awakening *Manipura* Chakra

Manipura chakra is situated behind the navel and symbolised as a bright yellow lotus with ten petals. Within the lotus is a red triangle representing agni tattwa, the fire element. The *bija mantra* for *Manipura* chakra is Ram, its colour is yellow and it is here that samana energy is governed, the energy responsible for processing all that we take in, transforming it into nourishment for the body and mind.

Manipura, the third chakra, translates as 'city of shining petals'. When awakened, it is bright and shining and we are full of vitality. It is linked to the sense of sight and we can often see its energy shining in the sparkle of the eyes. Known as the solar plexus, it is our own little sun, our 'inner fire' or 'vital spark'. It is where we hold a lot of our 'gut feelings' and in the physical body, the network of nerves in the solar plexus is often referred to as the second brain, our body's unconscious intelligence from where we can be guided, if we are able to tune in. It is also the centre of self-assertion and will-power and associated with ambition and confidence. *Manipura* is linked to transformation, our ability to face life's many challenges, to rise from the ashes, learn from our experiences and use them to change and move forwards positively.

Physically, it is chiefly concerned with digestion and the drive to nurture oneself. The main associated gland is the pancreas, producing hormones to break down our food, though it is also linked to the outer adrenals which produce hormones to help convert food into energy. *Manipura* governs the functioning of the whole abdominal area, including the liver, stomach and upper intestines as well as the mid back and spine.

Sluggishness and lethargy can indicate low energy in *Manipura*, when the agni fire of digestive energy becomes weak and we lose the ability to draw nourishment from our food. When the chakra is open we are able to tune into other people's energy and can be sensitive to their needs. If it is too open however, we can become overly concerned with the needs of others at the expense of our own and the energy we need to nurture ourselves is 'leaked' out or given away, leaving us drained and tired. When *Manipura* energy is too high, digestive energy is excessive, with the risk of ulcers, heartburn and even diabetes developing. Psychologically, we become overly focused on our personal power to the detriment of others' needs and are prone to impatience and angry outbursts.

Qualities Associated with a Balanced Third Chakra

When *Manipura* energy is balanced we are likely to show integrity, perseverance and passion in the activities and the people we commit to. We are unafraid to assert ourselves and claim our own personal power, whilst remaining open to others' needs, opinions and views. Boundaries between ourselves and others are healthy and clear, self-esteem is good and we are likely to take stock of our inner feelings before making decisions, reflecting a sense of self-discipline, an ability to wait, digest experience and then act accordingly. We may adopt a leadership role, with others drawn to our charisma and vitality. We have good energy levels as our digestive fire is strong, allowing us to draw nutrition from the food we eat and the air we breathe. We are able to nurture the body and respond to its physical needs and in doing so are more able to generate and focus energy on the activities and people we value.

Problems Associated with an Imbalanced Third Chakra

With an imbalance in *Manipura*, there may be a sense of powerlessness or a need to dominate. A healthy, integrated sense of self and identity is lacking and as such, is sought out through relationships with others, with the resulting need to manipulate and control, or become dependent and overly passive. Vanity, pride and egocentric behaviour may be present and the individual can appear arrogant and superior in their dealings with others. Experiences and feelings are unable to be fully digested, so we tend to act upon impulse with the risk of socially irresponsible or hyperactive behaviour developing. On a physical level, imbalanced third chakra energy may manifest in disorders of the stomach, abdominal organs and digestive system. Eating disorders and low energy problems such as chronic fatigue are also linked to *Manipura* imbalance.

How to Awaken *Manipura* Chakra

Breathing

Kapalabhati Pranayama (breath of fire)

- Sit in *Vajrasana*, kneeling posture, with the shins and front of the feet gently pressing into the floor (alternatively place a folded blanket between the thighs and calves if needed, or sit in a chair). Lengthen the neck and spine and place the palms of the hands on the knees.
- Take a few even breaths and relax the belly.
- Exhale strongly through both nostrils whilst drawing the navel area firmly to the back of the body.
- Allow the following inhalation to take place passively by allowing the abdominal muscles to relax.
- Focus on the movement of the breath in the belly, ensuring the shoulders and face remain relaxed throughout.
- *Kapalabhati* is a rapid breathing exercise, roughly one second for each exhale and one second for each passive inhale.
- Begin with 10 to 15 breaths per cycle, take a few balanced resting breaths and repeat for two more cycles. Over time, the number of breaths per cycle can gradually be increased to 40 to 60. Afterwards, take a few minutes to

allow the breath to return to an even rhythm and focus on the after-effects of the practice which may include increased heat and energy within the body and a tingling sensation in the skin.

Benefits: Strengthens and cleanses the respiratory system, helps regulate the metabolism and tones the digestive organs. It is also a cleansing exercise for the *nadis* and has an energising effect on the mind and body. (Avoid *Kapalbhati* during pregnancy or periods and if there are heart problems, high blood pressure or gastric problems).

***Uddiyana Bandha* (abdominal lock)**

- Sit in *Vajrasana*, kneeling posture, with the spine lengthened, the body relaxed and place the palms of the hands on the knees.
- Take a long, deep breath through the nostrils then exhale slowly and fully through the nostrils, drawing the abdomen back towards the spine.
- Hold the breath outside, press the palms to the knees, straighten the arms and lower the head, lengthening the back of the neck.
- Pull the abdominal muscles further towards the back of the body and draw them upwards inside the lower ribs.
- Hold the abdominal lock and the breath for a few seconds, without straining, and with practice build up to 5 to 10 seconds.
- Release the abdomen, relax, raise the head and breathe in.
- Repeat another two to three times, taking a few resting breaths between each practice.

Benefits: *Uddiyana bandha* stimulates *Manipura* and improves the functioning of the digestive organs. (Avoid this practice during pregnancy and periods or if there are gastric problems such as ulcers or hernia).

Physical Exercises

Supta Pawanmuktasana (leg lock pose)

- Lie down on the floor with your spine and legs lengthened.
- Bend the right leg, draw the thigh and knee as close to the chest as you can whilst keeping the left leg lengthened. Place the hands over the knee, interlace the fingers and as you exhale, draw the knee towards the chest, the thigh to the belly and the belly to the spine.
- Keeping the left leg and the back on the floor, breathe in slowly and raise the head and shoulders, drawing the chin to the throat and the forehead to the knee.
- Hold your breath for a short time in the raised pose, then exhale slowly and lower the head and shoulders to the floor, keeping the chin drawn in and back of the neck long.
- Repeat, three to five times, then straighten the bent leg and relax the body.
- Repeat the same number of rounds for the left leg.

Benefits: Strengthens the lower back muscles, massages the abdomen and digestive organs and relieves indigestion and constipation. (Avoid if there are serious back problems).

Navasana (boat pose)

- Sit in *Dandasana* with the spine lengthened, sitting bones gently pressed down and the legs extended. Bend the knees and place the feet together on the floor.
- Lean back slightly and balance on the sitting bones. As you exhale, draw the navel back and raise the shins parallel to the floor.
- Balance on the sitting bones as you lengthen the arms out in front of you, palms facing each other, collarbones wide and shoulders-blades drawn down the back.
- Keep the spine and neck lengthened and lift and open the chest and heart. Keep focused on the breath, expanding the rib-cage as you breathe in, drawing the belly and abdominal organs back as you breathe out.
- Remain in the pose for a few breaths, slowly building up to ten breaths. When you feel ready for the full posture, lengthen the legs out so the body forms a v-shape

Benefits: Strengthens the abdominal muscles, the legs, back and spine and stimulates the digestive system.

***Ardha Matsyendrasana* (half kingfish twist)**

- From *Dandasana*, bend the right leg and cross the right foot over the left leg, placing the right foot flat on the floor just above the outside of the left knee.
- Root the sitting bones down, place the right finger-tips on the floor, just behind the spine and gently press down with the fingers to lengthen the spine. Allow the top of the head to rise to the ceiling with the chin parallel to the floor.
- Raise the left arm above the head and lengthen from the waist to the fingertips.
- Exhaling, draw the navel and lower abdomen in and begin to revolve the abdomen and rib-cage to the right. Place the left elbow around the outside of the right knee, drawing the right knee and thigh to the abdomen. Bend at the elbow with the palms facing forwards, fingers pointing upwards.
- Turn the head to look along the right shoulder and lengthen the right shoulder and collarbones to the wall behind.

- Stay in the posture for five to ten slow, even breaths. With each inhale lengthen the spine and with each exhale gently draw the belly in and allow the abdomen to twist a little more, as though the waist were a cloth that you were 'wringing out'.
- Slowly untwist, feeling the spine lengthening then repeat on the left side.

Benefits: Massages and tones the abdominal organs. (Avoid in pregnancy and the first few days of periods).

Saithalyasana (animal relaxation pose)

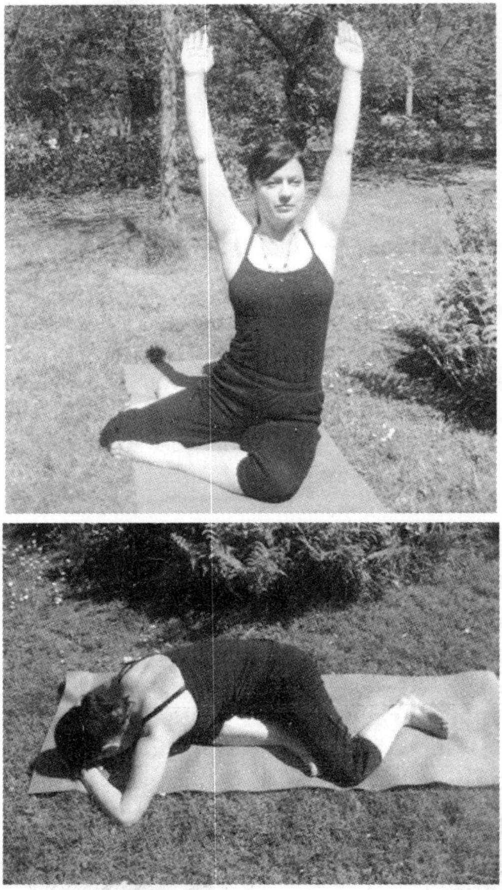

- Sit in *Dandasana*, with the legs lengthened and the sitting bones rooted down.
- Bend the right leg and place the sole of the foot on the inside of the left thigh, just above the knee, releasing the right knee and leg to the floor.
- Bend the left knee, internally rotate the hip and thigh-bone and take the left leg back, allowing the knee to release to the floor and the lower leg and foot to rest behind the back.
- Turn the belly to face the right thigh with the arms by the sides.
- Raise the arms above the head as you inhale and as you exhale, bend forwards over the right knee, resting the forehead onto the backs of the hands.
- Stay for a few breaths focusing on the belly gently pressing down on the thigh as you inhale.
- To come out of the pose, breathe in, press the hands down and raise the arms and the trunk. Repeat two to three times and on the final pose rest the belly on the thigh for ten breaths or so, then repeat on the other side.

Benefits: Opens the hips and lower back, massages the abdominal organs and induces relaxation.

Yogamudrasana (psychic union pose)

- Sit cross legged and close the eyes.
- Take both arms behind the back and hold the wrist of one arm with the other hand.
- Breathe in deeply and as you exhale, slowly bend forward, taking the forehead towards or onto the floor (use a cushion or folded blankets to rest the forehead if it does not come to the floor comfortably).
- Stay for as long as feels comfortable, focusing on the gentle rhythm of your breath.
- Slowly return to the starting position on an inhale then repeat the pose with the legs crossed the other way around and the other hand holding the wrist.

Benefits: Massages the abdominal organs, improves digestion, opens the back muscles and hips and induces relaxation.

***Jathara Paravritti* (reclining abdominal twist)**

- Lie down with the spine lengthened and the knees bent, feet together and flat on the floor.
- Exhale and draw the knees to the chest, keeping the lower back relaxed and open.
- Lengthen the arms out at shoulder level, palms facing upwards, collarbones and backs of the shoulders wide.

- Inhale and expand the rib-cage, lift the hips up slightly and as you exhale, keep the legs and feet together and roll the knees towards the right elbow, softening the belly.
- Release the back of the left shoulder and shoulder-blade to the floor and turn the head to look along the left arm, drawing the chin to the shoulder, keeping the neck long.
- Stay for five slow breaths and gently twist the belly and waist a fraction more with each exhale, drawing the knees closer to the right elbow and revolving the rib-cage and upper body to the left. Engage the abdominals, inhale and draw the knees back to centre and repeat on the left side.
- To avoid any pressure on the abdomen, for a more gentle twist, keep the soles of the feet on the floor and roll onto the edges of the feet, lengthening the lower spine.

Benefits: Massages the abdominal organs, strengthens the abdominal muscles and improves flexibility in the hips and spine. (The gentler version can be done during pregnancy and periods).

Agnisaar Kriya (cleansing the fire)

- Sit in a comfortable seated posture with the spine lengthened.
- Breathe in deeply and breathe out completely, drawing the abdomen back to expel as much air as possible from the lungs.
- Hold the breath out, then draw the abdominal muscles back and move the head down so the chin draws towards the chest (if you have neck or upper back pain do not move your head down and instead look straight ahead).
- Release the abdominals then draw them back again and continue to do so, drawing the navel area back and forth, whilst holding the exhaled breath, without straining (five or six times is fine to begin with.)
- Raise the head, relax, and breathe in. Take several, balanced resting breaths and repeat up to three times. With practice, the abdominals will strengthen and the

number of times you can contract and release the navel whilst holding the breath will slowly increase.

Benefits: Stimulates agni, the fire element and energy of digestion, massages the abdominal organs and helps improve energy levels. Always practice on an empty stomach. (Avoid in pregnancy, periods or if there are any abdominal complaints, heart problems or high blood pressure).

Relaxation

Rest for five minutes in *Shavasana* (as outlined in *Mooladhara* chapter) focusing on the breath and allowing the body to feel the benefits of your practice.

Meditation

Sit in a comfortable cross legged posture with the sitting bones rooted down and the spine lengthened. Place the hands in *Rudra mudra*, the fire *mudra*, by placing the tips of the thumbs, the index fingers, and the third fingers together. Extend the middle and little fingers and place the backs of the hands on the knees, palms open and facing upwards.

Visualise a circle of bright yellow light, gently spinning (horizontally and clock-wise) in the belly or solar plexus. Feel this light shine like a golden sun within. Breathe in to the belly and as you breathe, visualise this light becoming brighter and clearer. Connect to the element of fire, to the qualities of inner strength and power. Stay with the practice for several minutes and each time your awareness wanders off with your thoughts, gently draw it back to the breath. With practice build up to ten minutes or more. Silently affirm 'I embrace my strength and power. I use them for my own and for the greater good'. Chant RAM (pronounced r-a-u-m) ten times on an exhale, slowly breathing in between each chant and focus on warm energy in the solar plexus becoming clear and bright. Sit quietly for a few minutes, noticing any after-effects of your practice.

Activities to Strengthen *Manipura* Energy

Eat slowly and with awareness, savouring your food and practising moderation in what you eat. Choose foods which nourish you and reduce the amount of processed food in your diet. Drink water regularly.

Trust your gut feelings and instincts. Slow down, take a breath and listen to your inner feelings. Take time to 'digest' your thoughts, rather than simply responding and acting upon them. Similarly, listen to and digest what others are expressing through their words and actions.

Learn to say no and to look after your own needs in relationships where you have adopted a passive role. Re-claim your personal power, both in your relationships and within society, by joining a pressure or activist group for a cause you believe in. Let go of the need to control or dominate others if you have adopted this role with friends, family or work-mates.

Learn to express anger appropriately and let go of long held resentment or bitterness. Practice forgiveness, both for yourself and for others you believe have hurt or wronged you.

Spend time in sunshine, enjoying its warm rays on your skin, whilst ensuring your skin isn't over exposed or under-protected.

Enjoy the warmth of an open fire or simply light some candles in your home and enjoy their warm, relaxing light.

11

Awakening *Anahata* Chakra

Anahata Chakra is situated in the heart area and symbolised by a blue lotus with twelve petals. In the centre of the lotus is a hexagon with two interlacing triangles, representing the air element, vayu tattwa. The *bija mantra* for *Anahata* Chakra is *Yam* and its colour, green. In *Anahata*, vyana energy is predominant, which governs the movement of energy throughout the body, responsible for the distribution and circulation of oxygen, food, and *prana* to where it is needed.

Anahata Chakra is the fourth energy centre, located in the heart centre and associated with the whole range of emotions we experience in our relationships, from jealousy to unconditional love. *Anahata* means 'un-struck', or 'stillness' and is thought to hold *anahata nada*, the sound of the universe itself, heard in deep meditation. It is also the centre associated with the sense of touch, with the hands and with giving and receiving. As this centre is awakened and the energy purified, feelings of compassion and acceptance begin to grow. We develop a greater sense of connection to others as well as an increased understanding of our own human frailty. *Anahata* is the centre of the chakra system and serves to allow the energy from the higher chakras to be expressed through our actions, whilst also allowing the energy from the lower chakras to move to a higher plane of awareness.

On a physical level, *Anahata* links to the chest, heart and lungs, to our circulation and to the upper back and shoulders. It is associated with the thymus gland, positioned in the upper part of the chest, behind the sternum. This gland is particularly active in childhood, and though it continues to grow throughout puberty, the gland then begins to diminish in size. An important role of the thymus is to process lymphocytes, essential to cellular immunity. That children have love, care and security through infancy and into their teenage years, to prepare them for life as independent beings, is something we take as a given when understanding their emotional and social development. The same principles apply physically, that the thymus gland develops fully, allowing the immune system to do the same, enabling the individual to physically function in the world, protecting their body from harm. The thymus and the heart chakra both have a need to be strengthened during childhood to form the secure, strong basis from which we can grow into adulthood, able to step out into the world with physical and emotional resilience, confidence and strength, caring for ourselves and able to care for and form loving attachments and relationships with others.

Qualities Associated with a Balanced Fourth Chakra

When the heart centre is balanced we are able to give and receive love. We can function independently and allow others to do so too. Our love is unconditional and we are often an inspiration to others, adopting a calm, kind and harmonious approach to life, with an attitude of gratitude for all that we experience. We see challenging events as an opportunity to grow and learn, are able to forgive ourselves and others and we trust in our path in life, moving onwards with hope and optimism. Physically, health is likely to be robust, with enjoyment of fresh air and the natural environment.

Problems Associated with an Imbalanced Fourth Chakra

With the heart centre imbalanced, our relationships and attachments may be possessive, insecure and co-dependent. We may fear abandonment and experience loneliness, as our relationships are likely to falter. Negative and critical thoughts are dominant and we tend to look for fault and apportion blame, rather than seeing the positive qualities in ourselves and others. We may withdraw from others, fearing being hurt, becoming defensive and aggressive to protect ourselves. An obsessive approach to admired figures may occur, behaviour often characterised in childhood and adolescence, which remains into adulthood if our heart energy is undeveloped. Depression may be present, as hopelessness, sorrow, pessimism, lack of self-love and a sense of alienation from others are experienced. Physically, heart, lung and respiratory problems may occur as well as upper back and shoulder problems.

How to Awaken *Anahata* Chakra

Breathing

***Bhastrika Pranayama* (bellows breathing)**

- Sit in a comfortable position, with the spine lengthened and sitting bones rooted down. Place the hands on the sides of the ribcage with the thumbs to the back of the body.
- Breathe in through the nostrils, widening the rib-cage into the fingers and thumbs, lifting the chest and stretching the diaphragm, to create maximum space for the lungs to expand.
- Confine the movement to the rib-cage, keeping the abdominal area still. Breathe out through the nostrils, drawing the sides of the rib-cage together to fully expel air from the base of the lungs.
- Allow the breath to find a comfortable rhythm, inhaling to a count of two, holding the inhale for a count of two and exhaling to a count two. Begin with one minute and gradually build up to two to three minutes. Relax and allow the breath to return to a steady, even rhythm.

Benefits: Strengthens the lungs and respiratory system, purifies the blood and helps calm the mind. (If there is high blood pressure or heart conditions, make the breath gentler and do not hold the breath).

Physical Exercises

Tadasana Gomukhuasana (mountain pose with arms in cow's face)

- Stand in *Tadasana* with the spine lengthened and feet grounded.
- Raise the right arm above the head with the palm facing the wall behind. Lift and lengthen the arm up and out from the shoulder. Bend the right elbow and draw the right forearm and palm down behind the head, towards the space between the shoulder-blades, palm on the upper back.

- Take the left arm out at shoulder level, rotate the arm so the palm faces the wall behind, bend the left elbow and draw the back of the left hand up the back towards the space between the shoulder-blades. With practice, the fingertips of the hands will draw closer to each other until you can hook the right fingers over the left.
- Keep the right upper-arm lifting up, the left upper-arm drawing down and the forearms and elbows drawing towards each other diagonally.
- Lengthen the neck, lift and open the chest, and breathe into the chest and rib-cage for five breaths (with practice build up to ten to fifteen breaths). Slowly release the arms and repeat on the other side.

Benefits: Alleviates neck problems, improves breathing by opening the chest, strengthens the knee joints and improves posture.

***Dwikonasana* (double angle pose)**

- Stand in *Tadasana* pose, take the feet hip width apart and parallel, with the spine lengthened.
- Take both arms behind the back, interlace the fingers and draw the backs of the hands towards the floor, opening the chest and widening the shoulders and collar-bones as you breathe in.
- Bend forward from the hips until the body and face are parallel with the floor.
- Raise the arms behind the back, without over-stretching and breathe into the upper chest, collar-bones and shoulders, lifting the backs of the hands to the ceiling. Stay for up to five breaths.
- To come out of the pose, lower the arms to the back, inhale and return to the upright position.
- Repeat up to five times.

Benefits: Improves breathing by opening the chest, strengthens the muscles between the upper spine and the shoulder blades as well as strengthening the shoulders, chest and neck.

***Tadasana Paschima Namaskar* (mountain pose with hands in prayer)**

- Stand in *Tadasana*, spine lengthened, with sides of the feet together, soles of the feet rooted down and the arms by the sides.
- Rotate the arms outwards as you inhale and inwards as you exhale, four or five times, then take them behind the back and join the palms and fingers, with fingertips pointing to the floor.
- Rest the thumbs on the lower back.
- Move the elbows back and rotate the wrists, so that the fingertips turn and point first toward the back and then upwards (if this proves difficult at first, hook the thumbs to the inside of the opposite elbow and have the lower arms parallel to the floor).
- Press the palms together and move them up the back until they are between the shoulder blades, breathing into the heart, chest, collarbones and shoulders.
- Draw the elbows down, to lengthen the upper arms and focus on keeping the chest and armpits open and the collar-bones wide. Keep the neck and shoulders relaxed. Breathe evenly into the chest for up to ten breaths.

Benefits: Improves posture and breathing, strengthens the upper body and alleviates neck problems. It also increases flexibility of the upper body, the arms, elbows and wrists.

***Parsvottanasana* (intense chest stretch)**

- From the pose above (with the hands behind the back in prayer posture or with the thumbs hooked inside the opposite elbow) turn the left foot slightly out and step forward with the right leg, as far as comfortable without losing balance.
- Inhale, opening the chest, widening the collar-bones and drawing the shoulder-blades down the back and prepare to bend forward.
- Exhale and bend forward over the right leg. Tuck the chin in to lengthen the back of the neck and hold for several breaths, lengthening the sitting bones and tail-bone to the wall behind and drawing the abdominals to the back of the body. Breathe into the heart, chest and collar-bones. Keep the sole of the front foot rooted down to the floor for balance.
- Inhale and slowly stand upright again. Repeat the pose with the left leg stepping forward.

Benefits: Improves flexibility in the neck, spine, shoulders, elbows and wrists, strengthens the abdominal organs, and opens the hips.

Ushtrasana (camel pose)

- Kneel on the floor with the knees hip width apart and the arms by the sides. Come up onto the shins, with the thighs perpendicular to the floor.
- Tuck the toes under and come onto the balls of the feet, releasing the tailbone down to the space between the heels.
- Inhale, draw the hips forwards, lift and open the chest, lean backwards slowly and reach for the right heel with the right hand then the left heel with the left hand. (If the hands cannot reach the heels, rest the palms on the back of the pelvis, fingers facing down and thumbs around the sides of the body).
- Lengthen and open the thighs and hips and bend the head and spine backwards as far as is comfortable. Gently press the hands onto the heels, keeping the arms strong and the shoulders supported, arching the upper back and breathing gently without over-straining. (With practice the pose can be deepened by un-tucking the toes and resting the tops of the feet and the shins on the floor and taking the hands to the soles of the feet).
- Inhale and slowly return to an upright posture, then take the hips to the heels and rest the body down over the thighs into child's posture.
- Only stay in the pose for as long as is comfortable or stay for only two to three breaths and repeat up to three times.

Benefits: Increases the capacity of the lungs, strengthens the back and the thighs and improves flexibility of the shoulders, neck and spine. (Avoid if there are back or neck problems, high or low blood pressure or migraines.)

***Utthan Pristhasana* (lizard pose)**

- Lie on the stomach, lift the chest and place the forearms on the floor in line with the chest. Hook the thumbs into the opposite elbow and place the fingers around the upper arms, just above the elbows.
- Have the legs hip-width apart and the front of the feet resting on the floor.
- Lift the trunk and buttocks around six inches from the floor and come onto the knees, keeping the elbows and forearms gently pressing down into the floor and the face looking forwards.
- Inhale, take the torso back and draw the chest and chin down towards the floor behind the forearms, allowing the chest to open and stretch, the upper arms to lengthen and the upper back to arch. Feel the heart opening and release it to the floor, keeping the elbows and forearms in the same position.
- Stay for 5 to 10 breaths, then lift the chest and chin as you inhale, return to the starting position, then repeat the posture two to three times.
- Lie down on the stomach to rest and focus on the effects of the posture.

Benefits: Opens and strengthens the chest, heart and diaphragm and improves flexibility in the shoulders, back and spine. (Avoid if there are serious back, shoulder or neck problems).

Relaxation

Rest for five minutes in *Shavasana* (as outlined in *Mooladhara* chapter) focusing on the breath and allowing the body to feel the benefits of your practice.

Meditation

Sit in a comfortable cross legged posture with the sitting bones rooted down and the spine lengthened. Join the tips of the thumbs and index fingers in *Gyan Mudra*, the air *mudra*. Place the backs of the hands on the knees and lengthen the other fingers, whilst opening the palms. See this as a gesture of openness, ready to receive and accept from a higher source.

Take awareness to the heart centre and visualise a sparkling emerald green circle of light, spinning horizontally and clockwise. Feel this light shining and as you breathe into the heart, feel the light become clearer and brighter. Connect to the element of air, to lightness and freedom and to the quality of love. Stay with the practice for several minutes and each time your awareness wanders off with your thoughts, gently draw it back to the breath. With practice build up to ten minutes or more. Silently affirm 'I am able to give and receive love. I invite love into my life'. Chant YAM (pronounced y-a-u-m) ten times on an exhale, slowly inhaling between each chant and focus on openness, warmth and compassion in the heart chakra, its light becoming pure and clear. Sit quietly for a few minutes noticing any after-effects of your practice.

Activities to Strengthen *Anahata* Energy

Take time to nurture and care for your physical body, eating healthy, enjoyable foods, walking in nature and breathing fresh, clean air.

Practice gratitude on a daily basis by reviewing three things you are grateful to have received or experienced that day, no matter how small. With practice, you will begin to notice more and more, small and previously un-noticed events, with gratitude.

Be compassionate and forgiving in your approach to other people and to yourself. Be aware of and challenge, the negative, harsh and critical thoughts you may harbour in your attitude to yourself and others.

Express feelings of love and be affectionate towards those you care about.

Volunteer. Choose to give your time to help those less fortunate than you.

Be kind. Practice small acts of kindness to those you encounter in day to day life. A smile or encouraging word to a friend or a stranger can be helpful to you both.

12

Awakening *Vishuddhi* Chakra

Vishuddhi chakra is situated in the base of the throat and is symbolised by a violet lotus with sixteen petals. In the centre of the lotus is a white circle representing *akasha tattwa*, the ether or space element, which is present within and between every cell in the body and through every part of the universe. The *bija mantra* for *Vishuddhi* chakra is *Ham* and its colour is blue. In *Vishuddhi*, the energy of udana is located, governing how we channel energy through the body, how we move and how we express our energy through our voice.

Vishuddhi translates as to 'purify' and is the centre for refining or purifying our energy. It processes the information and wisdom received from the higher chakras and allows us to express our emotions from the chakras below, so determines to what extent we can 'speak from the heart', with integrity and truth. It is linked to our sense of hearing, so is also about how well we can listen to others before responding.

On a physical level, *Vishuddhi* influences the health of the neck and throat, the thyroid and parathyroid glands, the mouth and jaw and the ears. The thyroid makes and stores hormones which help regulate the heart rate, blood pressure, body temperature and the rate at which food is converted into energy. As the master gland for metabolism, it is essential for balancing and regulating energy in every cell in the body, so our inner vibrancy and zest for life are determined by its health. *Vishuddhi* chakra helps us express this unique energy, so determines how we make our mark on other people and the world around us and how we manifest our potential.

Qualities Associated with a Balanced Fifth Chakra

When *Vishuddhi* is balanced we can communicate truthfully, clearly and honestly. We are concise in our speech and in how we approach our life, so are likely to be quite organised and disciplined. Often the ability to express can be creative, through singing, poetry and art. We are likely to be able to inspire others through our words and their expression and perhaps adopt a teaching role in our lives. We are also able to listen to and respect the words of others, so are more likely to make good judgements, not only by considering others' needs, but also by listening to our own inner voice. In doing so, our goals in life are more able to manifest and we have more clarity and as we travel our path through life.

Problems Associated with an Imbalanced Fifth Chakra

When *Vishuddhi* energy is imbalanced we may experience a range of physical symptoms linked to thyroid functioning and metabolism, such as fatigue, weight problems, insomnia, skin and hair changes (particularly hair loss), poor tolerance to cold, and in children, poor growth. Imbalance may also affect the voice, the ears, neck and throat, or manifest as mouth, gum and jaw problems.

On a mental and emotional level, imbalance will affect our ability to speak the truth or make clear decisions. We are unlikely to relax easily and may have difficulty expressing our needs, becoming passive and fearful in the face of obstacles. We may feel un-listened to, so avoid interaction with others, or our interactions may have little depth or true connection, consisting instead of gossip and chatter. There is a risk of hedonistic, avoidant behaviours developing, where we shut out connection with our feeling and emotions from the chakras below and the wisdom from the mind chakras above. This can lead to addiction problems, which will further compound the imbalance. We may exist in a state of denial, unable to see the truth or have any connection to our true feelings and inner voice.

How to Awaken *Vishuddhi* Chakra

Breathing

Ujjayi Pranayama (victorious breath)

- Sit comfortably with the spine lengthened and inhale slowly through the nostrils. Slightly contract the back of the throat as you breathe, creating a soft, low, hissing sound in the throat.
- Allow the sound to maintain a smooth, even quality and to emerge from the throat, rather than from the nose, as though you were drawing the breath in through the throat rather than the nostrils.
- Exhale slowly, keeping the body relaxed, focusing on the breath passing through the throat and keep the sound of the breath smooth and unbroken, with the breath rhythm steady and deep. Practice for one to three minutes, gradually building up to five minutes.

Benefits: *Ujjayi* is also known as the psychic breath. It induces deep relaxation, helps to relieve insomnia and headaches, slows down the heart rate, improves thyroid functioning and benefits the throat and the whole respiratory system.

Jalandhara Bandha (throat lock)

- Sit comfortably with the spine lengthened.
- Place the palms on the knees and allow the breath to deepen.
- Inhale slowly and hold the breath, take the head forwards and the chin to the chest.
- Keep the arms straight with the palms pressing the knees and draw the shoulders upwards and forwards, lengthening the back of the neck and pressing the chin to the chest.
- Hold the position for a few seconds, keeping the breath held in and feel the energy in the upper chest and throat expand. Gradually build up to 10 seconds, without straining or holding beyond your comfort level.

- Bend the elbows, relax the shoulders, gently unroll the head and breathe out slowly. Take a few, even, resting breaths. Repeat three times, focusing on purifying the energy in the throat centre.

Benefits: Massages the thyroid, so helps to balance and regulate the metabolism. It also helps reduce the heart rate whilst improving circulation and breath retention and induces mental relaxation.

Physical Exercises

Sethu Bandasana (bridge pose)

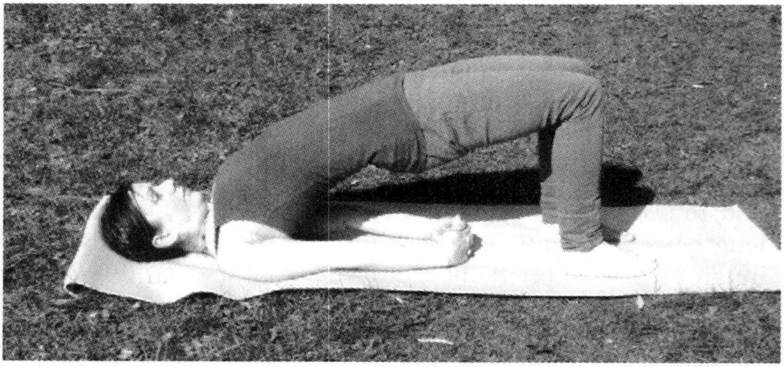

- Lie down on the back with the spine lengthened, arms by the sides, knees bent, feet hip-width apart and parallel and the shins perpendicular to the floor.
- Lift and spread the toes and feel the outer and inner edges of the feet root down into the floor with the arches lifted.
- Draw the pelvic floor muscles upwards, into the body and the abdominals back towards the spine.
- While inhaling, raise the hips and uncurl the spine from the floor. The head, shoulders and soles of the feet remain in contact with the floor and the arms and palms gently press down. Keep the back of the neck long and allow the breath to slow down, aware of the movement and the sound of the breath in the throat, as in *Ujjayi* breath. Stay for 5 to 10 breaths, feeling the spine lengthen and the front of the body open.

- As you become more familiar with the pose, lift the chest further to the chin, rotate the upper, inner arms outwards, then draw the arms underneath the body, interlace the fingers and draw the backs of the hands towards the feet.
- As you inhale, gently press the backs of the shoulders down and keep opening and lifting the chest. As you exhale, lengthen your thighs and knees to the wall in front and raise the hip-bones. Ensure the knees stay above the ankles and the feet, particularly the outer edges of the big toes, stay rooted into the floor.
- Exhale and slowly unroll the spine onto the floor vertebrae by vertebrae, lengthening the tail-bone to the space between the heels. Roll the knees to the right and then to the left, several times to release the spine, then lengthen the legs.

Benefits: Improves the functioning of the thyroid, opens and tones the abdomen and the female reproductive organs, lengthens the spine and opens the shoulders and chest. (Avoid in later stages of pregnancy, or if there are abdominal problems such as hernia or ulcer).

Supta Vajrasana (sleeping thunderbolt pose)

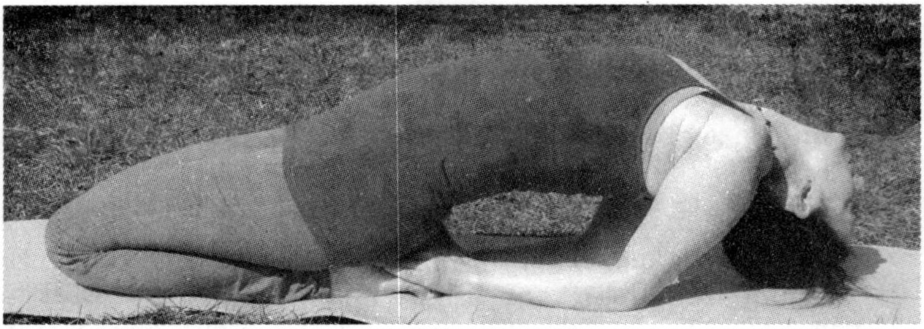

- In *Vajrasana* pose, kneel with the knees and ankles together, the hips resting on the heels, the shins and the front of the feet resting on the floor and the spine lengthened. Slowly lean back and place the palms down, fingers facing forwards.
- Lengthen the thighs and keep the knees facing forwards rather than rolling inwards towards each other.
- Bend the elbows and lower them towards the floor. Do not over-stretch. With practice, deepen the pose, with the forearms and elbows resting on the floor.
- Gently arch the back. Lower the body down and take the top of the head to rest on the floor.
- Keep the knees in contact with the floor and the thighs lengthened.
- Breathe slowly, focusing on openness in the throat, chest and heart. Stay for five breaths and over time slowly build up to 10 to 15 breaths.
- To come out of the pose, press the elbows and lower arms to the floor, slowly lift the head, draw the chin in to the throat so the neck is lengthened, use the hands to support you and return to *Vajrasana*, kneeling posture.

Benefits: Activates the thyroid, opens the chest (so is helpful in improving respiratory problems), massages the abdominal organs and helps increase flexibility of the neck, back and spine. (Avoid this *asana* if there are neck, back, or knee problems).

Halasana **(plough pose)**

- Lie on the back with the knees bent and the feet flat on the floor, legs and feet together.
- Engage the abdominal muscles, lift the legs over the head, raise the hips and lengthen the legs towards the wall behind.
- Stretch the soles of the feet to the wall behind and place the palms of the hands on the lower back for support.

- Draw the toes down towards the floor, only to your comfortable limit, without overstretching.
- Interlace the fingers behind the back and straighten the arms, gently pressing the shoulders into the floor, lengthening the spine and drawing the hips upwards.
- Keep the abdominals engaged and drawn to the back of the body and lift the pelvic floor muscles upwards and into the body.
- Keep the hips in line with the shoulders and breathe slowly and evenly, aware of the movement and sound of the breath in the throat, as in *Ujjayi* breath. Stay for 5 to 10 breaths.
- Roll out of the pose slowly, one vertebra at a time, keeping the legs lengthened. When the lower spine uncurls to the floor, bend the knees and take the feet to the floor. Gently roll the knees to the right, then to the left, releasing any tension in the back.

Benefits: Strengthens and stimulates the thyroid gland, improves blood circulation and opens and stretches the shoulders and spine. It is also very calming, helps reduce stress and fatigue and relieves backache, headache and insomnia. (Avoid in the first few days of menstruation, later stages of pregnancy, or if there are neck problems, back problems or high blood pressure).

***Vipareeta Karani Mudra* (half shoulderstand)**

- Lie down on the floor and draw the knees to the chest.
- Lift both legs up, engage the abdominals, lift the hips and bring the feet over the head.
- Place both hands behind the back, resting the palms on the lower back, fingers pointing upwards. Keep the elbows in line with the shoulders, upper arms parallel to each other and back of the neck lengthened.
- Keeping the chest wide and the shoulders grounded, unroll the back from the floor and allow the pelvis and hips to rest on the hands for support.
- Press the shoulders to the floor, engage the abdominals and leg muscles and keep lengthening the body upwards, with the feet in line with the eyes.
- Hold the pose for 5 to 10 breaths, focusing on the movement of the breath in the throat, as in *Ujjayi* breath. With practice, build up to holding the pose for three to five minutes.
- To come out of the pose slowly bend the knees towards the sides of the forehead and uncurl the spine, one vertebra at a time, down onto the floor. Lower the legs, then bend the knees and take the feet to the floor and roll the knees and legs to the right and then to the left a few times to release any tension in the back. Return to *Dandasana*.

Benefits: Stimulates the thyroid, strengthens the heart and lungs, calms the mind and revitalizes the body. (Avoid in the first few days of menstruation, later stages of pregnancy, or if there are high blood pressure, neck or back problems).

Matsyasana (fish pose)

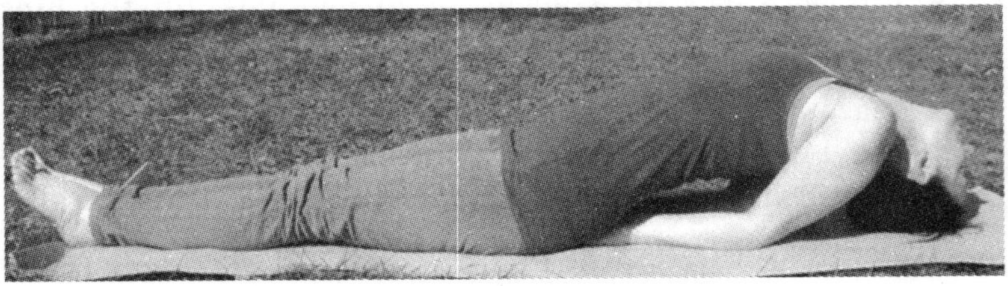

- Sit on the floor, in *Dandasana*, with the legs outstretched, feet and legs together and the spine lengthened.
- Lean back, lower the forearms and elbows to the floor, then draw the elbows and forearms towards each other and place the hands underneath the lower back, the fingers underneath the buttocks, with the palms down.
- Lift the chest, arch the back and slowly take the crown of the head to rest lightly on the floor behind, with the elbows, forearms and palms pressing down to support the back and spine, and open the chest.
- Breathe slowly, focusing on openness in the throat, chest and heart. Stay for five breaths and over time slowly build up to 10 to 15 breaths.
- To come out of the pose, press the forearms and elbows down strongly and slowly raise the head, drawing the chin to the throat to lengthen the back of the neck. Release the arms from under the body, return to *Dandasana* and circle the head to release any tension in the neck.

Benefits: Opens the chest, throat and abdomen, helps regulate the thyroid and the thymus glands, regulating the metabolism and boosting the immune system. (Avoid if there are heart problems or neck problems, or abdominal complaints such as hernia or ulcers).

Relaxation

Rest for five minutes in *Shavasana* (as outlined in *Mooladhara* chapter) focusing on the breath and allowing the body to feel the benefits of your practice.

Meditation

Sit in a comfortable cross legged position with the spine lengthened and the sitting bones gently pressed down into the floor. Place the thumbs on the pads of the middle fingers and the tip of the tongue on the roof of the mouth just behind the front teeth, in Akashi, the *mudra* of inner space. Extend the other fingers and rest the backs of the hands on the knees. Take awareness to your throat and visualize a circle of blue light, spinning horizontally and clock-wise in the base of the throat. Draw the breath into the throat and feel this light become clearer, a beautiful sky blue light. Connect to the element of space, to the space within your body, the space within the mind, the space between the earth and the planets and to the qualities of expression, truth and communication. Stay with the practice for several minutes and each time your awareness wanders off with your thoughts, gently draw it back to the breath. With practice build up to ten minutes or more. Silently affirm, 'I allow myself to speak my truth clearly and with confidence'. Chant HAM (pronounced h-a-u-m) ten times on an exhale, inhaling slowly between each chant, focusing on clearness in the throat, clarity in expression and throat energy becoming pure and clear. Sit quietly for a few minutes, noticing any after-effects of your practice.

Activities to Strengthen *Vishuddhi* Energy

Enjoy activities where you use your voice, such as singing, chanting, reciting poetry, reading aloud. Join a choir, a book club, poetry group, or a debating or political group to connect with others and express your views.

Take the time to listen to what others are saying before responding. Check with them that you have understood their meaning and respect their point of view, even if it clashes with your own.

Be aware of any tendencies to judge and criticize. Resist speaking negatively and critically of yourself and other people and refrain from complaining about events in your life.

Learn to say no, avoid people-pleasing and learn to express your needs clearly by taking an assertiveness course or a workshop in communication skills or public speaking.

Look after your metabolism by avoiding reliance on quick-fix energy lifts like caffeine and instead make slow release foods like oats, nuts and seeds, a part of your regular diet. Soothe an irritable throat with hot lemon and honey.

Avoid unnecessary chatter and gossip and take time each day to enjoy the sound of silence.

Enjoy listening to music. Enjoy listening to the sounds of nature, such as bird-song, the wind blowing through the branches of a tree, the sound of a flowing river, or of waves lapping to the shore of the sea.

Ensure you have enough sleep and make the hour or so before bed, a winding-down, relaxing routine, with your bedroom and bed a comfortable, peaceful sanctuary.

13

Awakening *Ajna* Chakra

Ajna chakra is situated behind the eyebrow centre and symbolised by a silver lotus with two petals, which represent the *Ida* and *Pingala nadis*. In the centre of the lotus is the sacred *bija mantra Om*. The element of this chakra is *buddhi*, the intellect, its colour is indigo and lilac and it is here that *prana* energy is governed. Given the same name as the universal life force, this energy helps us draw nourishment from the air around us, the breath and from all that we experience through our senses.

Ajna, also known as the brow chakra, translates as 'to not know', referring to the mind maintaining the illusion of ourselves as separate, individual beings rather than drawing upon the wisdom of the higher self, the 'knowing without words' of our connection to universal consciousness. It is where the *ida* and *pingala nadis* merge once more, after travelling upwards from *Mooladhara*. *Ajna* energy has the most influence over the personality and sense of identity and governs how we express our psychological characteristics and how we understand and channel our emotions, positively and creatively, for the greater good. Strengthening *Ajna* energy helps us strengthen the functioning of the mind, improving memory and concentration. It allows us to develop the inner power of *buddhi*, the higher mind, which enables us to discriminate between what is truth and what is illusion. It lifts the cloudiness of the mind, known as *Maya*, the veil of perception, enabling us to see the difference between our fear-based reactions and emotional responses, our habitual thoughts and beliefs and those based on our wisdom and innate intelligence. It is known as the 'sixth sense' and as such, it governs the organisation of the information from the five senses. It is also called the 'third eye' and is the doorway between the conscious and unconscious mind and between our intellectual and psychic abilities. Awakened, it brings the ability to witness without judgement and maintain awareness of the larger meaning and purpose of our experiences in life.

On a physical level *Ajna* is linked to the brain and nervous system, as well as the eyes, ears and nose. It connects to the pituitary gland, and to the pineal, which produce and regulate many hormones, essential for the functioning of the whole body. These glands oversee the functioning of the physical body just as *Ajna* chakra, when awakened, oversees, and brings control to the pranic or energy body. With *Ajna* energy in balance, we see clearly our path in life and are able to let go of fear and re-claim our strength and power as awakened, enlightened beings.

Qualities Associated with a Balanced Sixth Chakra

When *Ajna* is balanced, the individual is likely to have a calm and peaceful demeanour with good physical and mental health. They are able to pick up on the quality of energy around them, so are sensitive to their surroundings and are good judges of other people. Able to evaluate other people's behaviour and circumstance as well as their own psychological responses, they learn from their experiences and are more able to accept, rather than judge, their own and others reactions, so can be empathic and compassionate. They may also be imaginative, with highly developed intellectual abilities. They are able to plan for the future, so appear resilient and more in tune with their path in life. Whatever ups and downs they experience on that path, they can still remain aware of a larger dimension existing beyond the physical plane, so are hopeful, optimistic and open to new experiences.

Problems Associated with an Imbalanced Sixth Chakra

With *Ajna* unbalanced, a range of psychological issues may be present. When the energy is weakened, poor memory, a sense of disorientation and confusion and a lack of initiative may be present, a fear of anything unfamiliar. When the energy is excessive the individual may seem overly rational and intellectual, with rigidly held thoughts and beliefs. They may be so 'in their head' that they are not in touch with their physical body and become increasingly trapped in their own mind, unable to see how their behaviour is causing them problems. They may appear arrogant, egocentric and self-righteous and become over-controlling of both their own and others behaviour, fearful of letting down their guard and allowing intuition to guide them. Physically, there may be headaches, mental health problems, hormonal imbalances and insomnia. Awakening and re-balancing *Ajna* energy allows the person to tune in to their inner vision and goals and to become more in touch with their purpose and path in life.

How to Awaken *Ajna* Chakra

Breathing

Find a comfortable, seated posture with the sitting bones rooted down, spine lengthened and crown of the head rising to the ceiling. Become aware of the movement of the breath through both nostrils. Close your eyes. Feel the warmth of the breath in the nostrils as you exhale and the cooler breath as you inhale. Observe the quality of the breath in both nostrils, noticing any differences as the breath gently moves through each nostril. Notice the point where the nostrils meet. Retain a gentle focus for 10 to 15 breaths. Now visualise you are drawing the breath into the nostrils to the point where the nostrils meet, then drawing the breath down the spine, to the base of the spine. Exhaling, visualise the breath travelling back up the spine, to the point where the nostrils meet, then softly exhale through both nostrils. Take ten to fifteen soft, gentle breaths. Return to a balanced even breath and come to stand.

Physical Exercises

In *Tadasana*, with the sides of the feet together, gently widen the soles of the feet, open and spread the toes, and press the feet into the floor. Close your eyes and notice if the body sways, from side to side, and forwards and back. Begin to find the point of balance between the left and right foot, front and back, inner and outer edges of the feet. Draw the crown of the head to the ceiling so the spine lengthens, open and lift the heart, widen the collarbones and allow the shoulder-blades to draw down the back. Focus on symmetry and balance within the body.

***Tandavasana* (Lord Shiva's dance)**

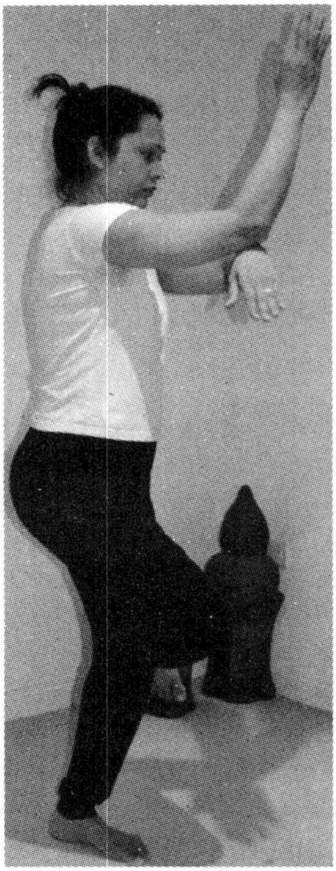

- Stand with feet hip width apart and parallel, with awareness on your breathing and focus on a fixed point on the floor in front.
- Shift your weight onto the right leg and gently press the sole of the right foot into the floor. Bend and lift the left knee, cross the left shin over the right knee and point the left foot and toes downwards, to the right of the right leg.
- Keep the right knee bent a little for better balance.

- Lift the right arm up to shoulder level, bend the elbow to a ninety degree angle and join the tip of thumb and index finger together to form *Gyan Mudra*, with the palm facing forwards.
- Lift the left arm up and place the back of the left wrist under the elbow of the right arm.
- Keep focused on your fixed point. Stay in the pose for three to five breaths, slowly building up to ten as you become more familiar with the balance, breathing deeply and keeping the focus between the eyebrows.
- Come back to *Tadasana* then repeat, with opposite arm and leg positions.

Benefits: Improves focus and concentration as well as strengthening the legs.

Garudasana **(eagle pose)**

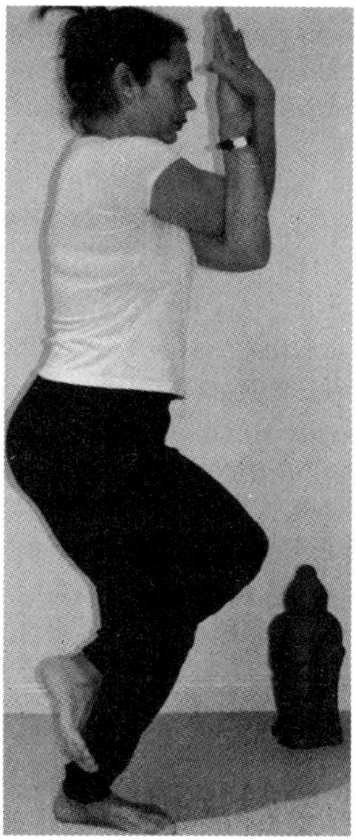

- Stand with feet hip width apart and parallel, with awareness on your breathing and focus on a fixed point on the floor in front.
- Bend the knees slightly, shifting your body weight onto the right leg and foot. Gently open the sole of the right foot and press it down, lift the left leg up and cross the left thigh over the right thigh.
- Point the left toes towards the floor, draw the foot back and hook the top of the foot behind the lower right calf.
- Now stretch the arms out to the sides and cross the right upper arm over the left, in front of the chest.
- Bend the elbows and with the right elbow in the crook of the left, raise the forearms to a ninety degree angle to the upper arms, wrap the forearms around each other, so the palms press together (alternatively press the backs of the hands together).
- Keep focused on your fixed point. Stay in the pose for three to five breaths, slowly building up to ten as you become more familiar with the balance, breathing deeply and evenly.
- When familiar with this pose try crouching eagle, by bending at the hips and knees, and drawing the elbows down towards the belly and the chin in towards the throat.
- To come out of the pose slowly unwind the legs, then the arms. Return to *Tadasana* and repeat on the other side.

Benefits: Improves concentration, strengthens the knees and legs and improves flexibility in the shoulders. Eagle posture also works on *Mooladhara* chakra, so helps us stay grounded when working with *Ajna*.

***Utthita Hasta Padangusthasana* (raised hand to big toe pose)**

- Stand with feet hip width apart and parallel, with awareness on your breathing and focus on a fixed point on the floor in front.
- When ready, shift your body weight onto the left leg, opening the sole of the foot and gently pressing it down.
- Bend the right knee and draw the thigh close to the chest. Draw the left kneecap upwards and hug the thigh muscles to the thigh bones. Gently draw the abdomen to the back of the body and focus on the steady rhythm of your breath.
- Hold the right big toe with the right fingers and thumb, hooking the index and middle fingers around the toe.
- Slowly start to stretch the right leg forward. If you are not able to stretch the leg fully then keep the knee slightly bent and focus on keeping the body steady and the spine lengthened.

- Lift the left arm out to the side at shoulder level and touch the thumb and index finger together in *Gyan mudra*. Breathe slowly, drawing the pelvic floor muscles upwards and the abdominals back.
- Keep your focus on your fixed point. Stay in the pose for three to five breaths. With practice, raise the left arm above the head and slowly build up to ten breaths as you become more familiar with the balance, breathing deeply.
- To come out of the pose bend the left knee, release the toe and slowly place the left foot on the floor.
- Repeat on the other side.

Benefits: Enhances concentration, strengthens the legs and hips and lengthens the hamstrings.

Eka Padasana **(one foot pose)**

- Stand with feet hip width apart and parallel, with awareness on your breathing and focus on a fixed point on the floor in front.
- Raise both arms up with the palms together and the thumbs crossed, fingers pointing upwards.
- Keep looking at your focus point and when ready, step your left leg forwards, take your weight onto the left leg and foot and gently press the foot to the floor.
- Draw the left kneecap upwards and hug the thigh muscles to the thigh bones. Gently draw the abdomen to

the back of the body and focus on the steady rhythm of your breath.

- Come onto the ball of the back foot and hinge forward from the hips, extending the right leg out behind you. Stretch the sole of the right foot to the wall behind and keep the arms extended, upper arms in line with the ears.
- With practice, the right hip and leg, the trunk and both arms are parallel to the floor in one strong, straight line.
- Keep your focus on your fixed point and hold the pose for three to five breaths, building up to 10, with practice. Slowly bend the standing leg, lower the back leg down and return to *Tadasana*. Repeat on the other side.

Benefits: Develops strength, co-ordination and concentration.

***Natarajasana* (dancer's pose)**

- Stand with feet hip width apart and parallel, with awareness on your breathing and focus on a fixed point on the floor in front.
- When ready, shift your weight onto the left leg and gently press the foot down. Bend the right knee and lift the right heel back towards the right buttock. Draw the left kneecap upwards and hug the thigh muscles to the thigh bones. Gently draw the abdomen to the back of the body and focus on the steady rhythm of your breath.
- Take your right arm back and hold the front of the right foot or the ankle with the right hand (alternatively loop a strap or tie around the ankle and hold with the hand).
- Hinge forwards from the hips and raise the left arm upwards, with the tips of the thumb and index finger together in *Gyan mudra*.
- Draw the right foot and shin back to the wall behind and press the back foot or ankle into the hand, whilst continuing to bend forwards, drawing the trunk and left arm more parallel to the floor.
- Keep focusing on your fixed point and breathe slowly for three to five breaths, building up to ten with practice.
- To come out of the pose slowly release the right foot to the floor, lower the arm, return to *Tadasana* and repeat on the other side.

Benefits: Improves concentration and balance, opens the hips and shoulders and strengthens the back, legs and arms.

Balasana (child's pose)

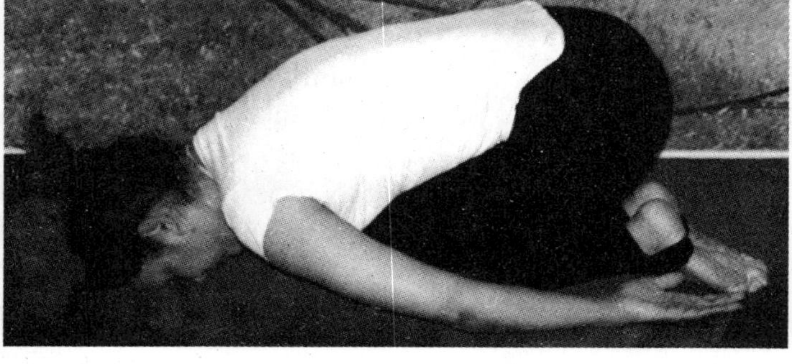

- Kneel down, with the hips resting on the heels and the front of the feet and shins resting on the floor.
- Bend forward from the hips and rest the forehead on the floor (or on a folded blanket or firm cushion, for height) in front of the knees, with the arms resting back by the sides of the body, the hands by the sides of the feet.
- Focus on the rhythm of your breath and the gentle pressure on the forehead. Gently breathe into the back of the rib-cage and feel the breath draw down to the base of the spine. Stay for ten to fifteen breaths then uncurl the spine from the mat.

Benefits: Induces relaxation, helps keep awareness on *Ajna* chakra as the forehead gently presses to the floor, yet also takes our awareness to *Mooladhara*, so helps to keep us grounded after working with *Ajna* energy.

Palming the Eyes

- Sit comfortably with the spine lengthened and rub the palms together rapidly until you feel increased heat and energy between the palms.
- Place the palms over the closed eyes, allowing the eyes to relax and enjoy the darkness and heat. When the heat from the palms fades repeat another one to two times.
- After the final time, rub the palms again then place them over the eyes with the eyes open and as you breathe in, feel you are drawing heat and energy into the eyes, re-vitalising and relaxing them.

Anulom Vilome (alternate nostril breathing)

- Sit comfortably with the spine lengthened.
- Take the tips of the index and middle fingers of the right hand to rest on the space between the eyebrows. Place the thumb next to the right nostril and the third and little fingers next to the left nostril.
- Keep the left hand in *Gyan mudra* (tip of the thumb and index touching) and place the back of the hand on the left knee.

- Close the right nostril with the thumb and breathe in slowly through the left nostril. Pause briefly then close the left nostril with the third and little fingers, open the right nostril with the thumb and exhale through the right nostril. Pause briefly.
- Inhale through the right nostril, close the right nostril with the thumb, pause briefly, open the left nostril, exhale slowly and pause.
- This constitutes one round. Begin with six rounds, focusing on the movement of the breath through the nostrils and the space between the eyebrows. With practice build up to ten rounds and allow the pause between each breath to lengthen.

Benefits: Induces relaxation and helps to remove health problems related to stress and anxiety. It also helps concentrate the mind and prepares it for meditation. Also known as *Nadi Shodhana*, it is a cleansing and purifying exercise for the *nadis*, helping to remove blockages in the energy channels.

Relaxation

Rest for five minutes in *Shavasana* (as outlined in *Mooladhara* chapter) focusing on the breath and allowing the body to feel the benefits of your practice.

Meditation

Place the hands in *Dhyani Mudra*, the gesture of meditation, by placing the back of the left hand in the right palm, with the tips of the thumbs touching and hands resting in the lap.

Take awareness to the space between the eyebrows and visualise a circle of indigo and lilac light, spinning (horizontally and clock-wise) inside the head. See this light become cleansed and bright as you draw your breath through both nostrils and into the space between the eyebrows. Focus on connecting with your inner wisdom. Stay with the practice for several minutes and each time your awareness wanders off with your thoughts, gently draw it back to the breath. With practice build up to 10 minutes or more. Silently affirm, 'I allow myself to see truth and follow my intuition'. Chant Om (pronounced a-u-m) 10 times, allowing the three syllables, to be clearly enunciated, and to flow into each other, inhaling slowly between each chant. Focus on the vibration within and on clarity and clear sight in the space between your eyebrows and visualise ajna energy sparkling and clear. Sit quietly for a few minutes, noticing any after-effects of your practice.

Activities to Strengthen *Ajna* Energy

Practice observing events, without reaction and without judgement, for 5 to 10 minutes per day. Simply witness what is happening as well as witnessing your own thoughts and emotions, with a sense of detachment and a curiosity and acceptance about what happens, rather than any expectations about how things should or ought to be.

In your day to day activities, keep drawing your attention back to the present moment and be aware when your focus has wandered with your thoughts into imagined future events, or dwelling on what has gone before. Each time, gently guide awareness back to the breath and to the present moment.

Practice candle-gazing, known as *Trataka* in yoga. Light a candle and sit around an arms length away, with the candle just below eye level. Stare into the flame and when your eyes tire, close them and imagine you can still see the flame in your mind's eye. When the eyes are rested, open them and return to gazing into the stillest point of the flame. Continue for five minutes, slowly building up to longer periods.

Each day take time to appreciate your positive qualities, strengths and abilities, no matter how insignificant you may judge them. Focus on these qualities becoming a larger part of who you are and put them into practice on a daily basis.

Develop your intuition by paying attention to inner guidance. Notice your habitual responses and reactions without judgement and beyond these, at a deeper level, learn to recognise and listen to a quieter voice within.

14

Awakening *Sahasrara* Chakra

Sahasrara, meaning 'one thousand' is situated at the crown of the head and represented as a shining lotus of a thousand petals. In the centre of the lotus is a shining light, the symbol of pure consciousness, beyond the elements of matter, time and space. Its colour is violet, with flashes of shining white light. Like *Ajna* chakra it links to the *Om Mantra*, though is chanted internally and silently, with the subtle vibrations of the silent chant helping us to connect to supreme stillness and peace.

Sahasrara links us to our higher selves and is the gateway to our relationship with the divine element. It is here that we can receive guidance in the form of thoughts, ideas and information, from the universal or infinite consciousness. As *Sahasrara* awakens, we begin to trust ourselves to be guided by these higher sources. The central *sushumna nadi* ends in *Sahasrara*, and with ida and *pingala* ending in *Ajna* chakra, it is at *Sushumna* that we can transcend the concept of duality and become aware of the inter-connectedness of all living things and of ourselves as multi-dimensional beings. *Sahasrara* is the entry point for divine energy to come into the body and give nourishment to physical, mental and emotional systems. It is from here that energy is distributed to the lower chakras.

Sahasrara links to the pineal gland and to the pituitary, both of which play a role in overseeing the functioning of the glandular system. The glands and the chakra have a 'meta' or transcendent role and are linked to states of consciousness, sleep rhythms, and the regulation of our mood. The delta waves associated with deep sleep are the same brain waves observed in states of deep meditation, where the meditator is conscious. Through the regular practice of meditation, the meditator may experience glimpses of the divine qualities of *Sahasrara*, such as bliss, joy and a sense of wonder at the universe. These states of mind may then begin to be experienced in day to day life, as our mood lifts and our whole system becomes more balanced. This is why the regular practice of meditation is so important in yoga, because when practiced regularly, the crown chakra aligns with universal energy, allowing us to be guided from a higher source and the functioning of the pituitary and pineal glands are strengthened, so helping to align the whole endocrine system and the mental and physical health of the entire body.

Qualities Associated with a Balanced Crown Chakra

When the crown chakra is balanced, the entire central nervous system has optimal functioning, allowing us to improve mental functioning such as memory, clarity of thought and the ability to see the bigger picture, or 'meta-perspective'. The higher functions of the mind are also developed and we become insightful and intuitive, fully living in the present, with openness, joy and spontaneity. We go with the flow of life, find wonder in the world around us, drawing inspiration from our environment and experiences. Our creativity increases and we also have more compassion for our environment and for all living things. As the body and mind become more balanced, through awakening *Sahasrara*, we may be perceived by others as having an inner light or inner glow as our energy system purifies and literally shines through the physical body.

Problems Associated with an Imbalanced Crown Chakra

Conversely when the crown chakra is imbalanced and the pineal and pituitary glands not functioning optimally, we may experience sleep problems, anxiety and depression and low energy levels. Fear and worry about the future are common and we lack the ability to change, adding to our sense of 'stuckness'. We experience ourselves as isolated from each other and from any connectedness to the earth or wider universe, so our sense of separation and loneliness are intensified. Our lack of spiritual awareness encourages excessive materialism and a lack of care for the welfare of others. An absence of creativity, narrow vision and a sense of purposelessness can combine to make our life seem a rather miserable and pointless experience, in comparison to the joyfulness associated with the balanced *Sahasrara*.

How to Awaken *Sahasrara* Chakra

Physical Exercises

Shasankasana (hare pose)

- Kneel on the floor, with the shins hip width apart and the thighs and spine vertical, arms by the sides.
- On an exhale, bend forwards from the hips to take the top of the head down onto the floor. Take the arms back and allow the backs of the hands to rest on the calves. Alternately, place the hands behind the knees, with the fingers lightly interlaced.
- Ensure the thighs are still in a straight line, with the hips in line with the knees. Stay for two to three minutes and focus on sensation in the crown of the head, breathing slowly and evenly.
- Uncurl on an inhale and sit on the heels, with the spine straight, focusing on any sensations in the body.

Benefits: Tones the legs, back and spine and with the head inverted, improves the blood supply to the brain, face and head, improving skin and scalp problems. (Avoid if there is high blood pressure).

Sirshasana **(half and full headstand)**
Head stand

Headstand is quite an advanced pose, so ensure you only move to Stages 2 and 3 when the previous stage can be held comfortably for three minutes or more.

Stage 1

- From kneeling, bend forwards, place the forearms down on the floor in front of you. Take the right hand over the inside of the left elbow and the left hand over the inside of the right elbow.
- Press the elbows and lower arms into the floor and interlace the fingers, keeping the elbows in line with the shoulders, so the arms form a triangular shape.
- Press the sides of the hands down and rest the crown of the head on the floor with an even distribution of weight between the forearms, elbows and crown of the head. Lengthen the neck.
- Come onto the balls of the feet and work towards straightening your legs. Press the balls of the feet down into the floor and walk the legs further into the body, aiming to have the spine vertical, tailbone and hips rising to the ceiling. Breathe evenly for two to three minutes, focusing on the spine and neck lengthening and the crown of the head gently pressing into the floor.

Stage 2

Practice against a wall at first, with the interlaced fingers two to three inches from the wall.

- From Stage 1, push the balls of the feet down and begin to raise the heels. Keep the spine lengthened and as you exhale, draw the pelvic floor muscles up into the body and the abdominals back towards the spine.
- Bend the knees, push the balls of the feet down and draw the knees to the chest, with the heels close to the buttocks. Breathe evenly, keeping the neck and spine lengthened and broaden through the back of the shoulders.

Stage 3

- From Stage 2, on an inhale raise the knees towards the ceiling, then straighten the legs, and raise the feet, with toes pointing upwards and body in a straight line.
- Keep the lower arms and elbows pressing downwards

and the shoulders lifting upwards, neck lengthened. Hold and breathe evenly.

- To come down, exhale and bend the knees, slowly lower the legs back down and rest in child's posture, with the forehead on the floor (or rest the forehead on the back of the hands) and the belly resting on the thighs.

Benefits: Builds stamina and strength and improves the functioning of the pituitary and pineal glands, bringing balance to the whole body and mind. The reversal of gravity revitalises the tissues and organs of the body. (Avoid if there are neck problems, headache or migraine, high blood pressure, heart disease, eye problems, or during pregnancy and periods).

Relaxation

Rest for five minutes in *Shavasana* (as outlined in *Mooladhara* chapter) focusing on the breath and allowing the body to feel the benefits of your practice.

Breathing: *Bhramari Pranayama* (humming breath)

- Sit comfortably in a cross-legged posture with the spine lengthened. Close the flaps of the ears with the thumbs and place the index fingers on the forehead, middle and third fingers over the eyes and little fingers under the eyes.
- Keep the elbows wide, the upper arms at shoulder level and the chest open.
- Breathe in through the nose and as you exhale, gently press the flat of the tongue to the roof of the mouth and make a humming sound, hmmmm . . . for as long as is comfortable, focusing on the vibration through the head and throat. Inhale slowly through the nostrils between each breath. Repeat 5 to 10 times.

Benefits: Induces calmness, quietens the mind, relieves anxiety, anger and insomnia. By chanting the third syllable of Om, mmm, we tune into the deeper realms of the mind and connect to universal consciousness.

Meditation

Sit comfortably with the spine lengthened and take the hands to *Shunya mudra*, known as heaven *mudra*, by bending the middle fingers of each hand into the base of the thumb and then lightly press the middle finger down, with the thumb. Extend the other fingers and place the backs of the hands on the knees.

Visualise the colour violet, with sparkling flashes of white light. Take attention to the crown of your head and imagine a circle of violet light, gently spinning horizontally and clockwise. Feel the crown of your head extending to the sky and as you breathe in, feel you are connecting to your higher self and to universal energy. Focus on the light becoming clearer and brighter. As you inhale, focus on the crown of the head drawing healing energy from the universe into the body, down to the base of the body and as you exhale, visualise that you are sending healing energy out into the world. Consciously let go of anything which may be blocking your connection to your higher self. Stay with the practice for several minutes and each time your awareness wanders off with your thoughts, gently draw it back to the breath. With practice build up to ten minutes or more. Silently affirm 'I draw guidance from the highest levels of love and light in the universe. I am connected to all that is good'. Chant Om (a-u-m) silently ten times, focusing on the vibration within, inhaling slowly between each silent chant, allowing the sound energy to help cleanse and balance your crown chakra and visualise your whole body filled with sparkling light. Sit quietly for a few minutes, noticing any after-effects of your practice.

Activities to Strengthen *Sahasrara* Energy

Take time each day to sit quietly and focus on the gentle rise and fall of the breath. Allow your awareness to connect to all living things, to the earth, the sky and the whole of the universe.

Spend time in appreciation of beauty, whether in nature, art, music or poetry, allowing your senses to be fully immersed. Be inspired and uplifted by your experience.

Allow day to day chores to develop a meditative quality, by being fully present with what you are doing. Devote tasks which you would rather avoid, to a higher power, adopting a selfless approach to your duties in life.

When faced with challenges, see the bigger picture. Instead of becoming caught up in the daily drama of life's events, stay focused on the larger meaning or purpose, with the positive approach of learning from all that you encounter.

See the good in yourself and in others. Remind yourself that each of us, in our sometimes very misguided ways, are all seeking to be loved and cared for.

Allow yourself to feel happiness and joy from the simple things in life, connecting to the innocence, playfulness and spontaneity enjoyed in childhood.

15

Chakra Breathing

Although we know that each chakra has its own qualities, connected to different aspects of our physical, mental and emotional functioning, we also know that together they form an energetic holistic system. For this to be active and in balance we can use a complete practice to work the whole system. The final four chapters outline practices which serve to 'fine tune' and balance the whole energy system. They can be used in conjunction with each other, with the warm up or with the individual chakra practices.

Chakra Breathing

By focusing the breath on the different energy centres and using specific breathing practices we can energise each chakra in turn. This is ideal for use on its own, or for times when a more active *asana* practice cannot take place for physical reasons, such as contra-indications, or simply practical reasons, such as lack of time or space. It can also be used to precede or end any of the other practices including the warm-up, the sun salutations and the individual chakra practices.

Sit in a comfortable pose with the spine lengthened and the sitting bones gently pressing down into the floor beneath. Sit on a *yoga* block or some folded blankets to raise the hips if there is any discomfort in the hips or lower back.

Close the eyes and relax the body. Take awareness to *Mooladhara* chakra. Breathe in and draw the perineum or pelvic floor area up into the body. Breathe out and relax. Repeat ten times then breathe gently and evenly for a minute or so, drawing the breath down into the base of the body and visualising *Mooladhara* clear and balanced.

Now take your focus to your lower abdominal area and *Swadhisthana* chakra. As you breathe in gently draw the lower abdominal muscles towards the back of the body. As you breathe out let go and relax the lower abdomen, aware of fluidity and flow within the body. Repeat ten times then breathe gently and evenly for a minute or so, drawing the breath down into the lower abdomen and visualising *Swadhisthana* clear and balanced.

Focus on the solar plexus and navel area and bring awareness to *Manipura* chakra. Breathe into the abdomen and as you breathe out, exhale through both nostrils as you strongly draw back the abdominal muscles. The following inhale involves no effort, instead just allows the abdominal muscles to relax. Continue for 10 to 15 breaths, feeling warmth in the solar plexus, then relax and take a few balanced, even breaths. Repeat two more times, then breathe gently and evenly for a minute or so, visualising *Manipura* clear and balanced. (Avoid in pregnancy, periods, or if there is high blood pressure, heart, or abdominal problems. Instead, just breathe into the navel area and gently draw the abdomen back as you exhale).

Take your focus to the heart area and to *Anahata* chakra. Begin to inhale by slowly expanding the ribcage. Feel the movement of the individual ribs outwards and upwards and be aware of this expansion drawing air into the lungs. Expand the chest and rib-cage as much as possible, whilst keeping the abdominal area still. Hold the breath for a few seconds. Exhale by relaxing the chest muscles and feel the sides of the rib-cage contracting, expelling stale air from the lungs. Continue for 10 to 15 breaths, feeling openness in the heart, then breathe gently and evenly for a minute or so and visualise *Anahata* clear and balanced.

Take your awareness to the throat and to *Vishuddhi* chakra. Gently contract the throat and begin to hear the breath passing through the throat as you inhale and exhale, producing a soft, low hissing sound, as though you were drawing the breath in and out through the throat and not through the nostrils. As the windpipe narrows, the sound of the breath becomes slightly louder. Take 15 to 20 slow breaths, then return to normal breathing for a minute or so, visualising *Vishuddhi* clear and balanced.

Take your focus between your eyebrows and awareness to *Ajna* chakra. Place the index and middle fingers lightly between the eyebrows. Close the right nostril with the right thumb and take a slow, even breath in through the left nostril. Close the left nostril with the third and little finger of the right hand and open the right nostril, to slowly breathe out. Breathe in through the right nostril then close it with the thumb, open the left nostril and breathe out. This completes one round. Continue for another nine rounds, breathing slowly and evenly, focusing on the space between your eyebrows, then release the fingers from the nostrils and breathe gently through both nostrils for a minute or so, visualising *Ajna* clear and balanced.

Bring awareness to the crown of the head and to *Sahasrara* chakra. Raise the arms, close the flaps of the ears with the thumbs and place the index fingers on the forehead, middle and third fingers over the eyes and little fingers under the eyes. Keep the elbows wide, the upper arms at shoulder level and the chest open. Breathe in through the nose and as you exhale, gently press the flat of the tongue to the roof of the mouth and make a humming sound, hmmmm....for as long as is comfortable, focusing on the vibration through the head and throat (the sound resembles the humming of a bee.) Inhale slowly through the nostrils between each breath. Repeat ten times, then release the hands and breathe evenly and slowly for a minute or so and visualise *Sahasrara* clear and balanced.

Relax and breathe evenly for a minute or so, visualising all of the chakras clear, balanced, and awakened and visualise bright, clear, shining energy flowing unobstructed within the whole body.

16

Surya Namaskar (Sun Salutation)

Sun Salutation is one of the oldest forms of flowing yoga sequences, traditionally practiced at sun rise. It was believed that the deep orange rays of the sun at this time stimulated the whole endocrine system and because the light is softer in the morning, it was more beneficial for the skin. Sun Salutation is an energising exercise, where we maintain focus on the breath rhythm as we move through each pose. It works the whole body in sequence, strengthening and opening the physical body, stimulating the energy centres and enhancing our awareness of the connection between the physical and pranic body and the subtle energy field within and all around us. It is also considered one of the cleansing practices in yoga, undoing and releasing knots of stagnant energy in the *nadis*, allowing energy to flow freely through the whole body. It can be used before any of the individual chakra practices, before the whole chakra breathing and meditation practices, or before the restorative practice. It is advised to begin with the warm up and practice on an empty stomach.

As Sun Salutation has several poses and involves moving from one pose to the next, it requires some level of flexibility and agility. For this reason it's advised to practice the poses individually before attempting the full Sun Salutation. In the beginning, the number of rounds should be three to four and as flexibility and strength improves, this can be increased to 6 to 12 rounds.

(Sun Salutations should be avoided if suffering from high blood pressure, heart disease or by those who have had a stroke. People with back conditions, hernia, abdominal problems or any other medical conditions are advised to consult their doctor before commencing this practice).

The Sun Salutation Practice

Awareness of each chakra

Before beginning, stand with the feet together and gently press the soles of the feet to the floor. Lengthen the spine, lift the top of the head and lift and open the chest. Gently draw the lower abdomen back and allow the tailbone to release to the floor. Balance the weight of the body equally between both feet, between the heels and balls of the feet and between the inner and outer edges of the feet. Visualise the whole body as one. As you inhale, imagine the breath reaching every single part of the body.

Focus on *Mooladhara* chakra. Visualise a bright red colour at the base of the body and breathe into the base for several breaths.

Slowly take your focus upwards and visualise *Swadhisthana* chakra as a bright orange colour shining in the lower abdomen and breathe into the lower abdomen for several breaths.

Move your awareness to *Manipura* chakra and visualise it as a bright yellow sun, warm and glowing in the belly and breathe into the solar plexus for several breaths.

Slowly move upwards and visualise *Anahata* chakra as a green shining light surrounding your heart. Feel your heart beating evenly and breathe into the heart area and chest for several breaths.

Now move your focus to *Vishuddhi* chakra. Feel the energy of *Vishuddhi*, as a sky blue light in your throat and breathe into the throat for several breaths.

Move your awareness to the space between your eyebrows. Visualise the indigo and lilac light of *Ajna* chakra between your eye brows, and draw your breath to the eyebrow centre for several breaths.

Feel the flow of energy moving upwards and gathering in the centre of your head. Visualise a sparkling violet light, with flashes of clear white light, shining brightly in the Crown chakra and feel a calmness and serenity as you breathe.

Relax and feel the whole of your body as one, gently expanding with each inhale, softening and releasing with each exhale.

Pose 1: Prayer pose (*Pranamasana*) Awareness on *Anahata* Chakra

Stand straight with both feet together and firmly grounded on the floor. Join both palms and place them in front of the chest with the thumbs gently pressing the centre of the heart area. Focus on the heart chakra and breathe in and out deeply.

Pose 2: *Hasta Utthanasana* (raised arms pose) Awareness on *Vishuddhi* Chakra

Breathe in as you raise both arms up over the head. Bend back slightly from the hips and tilt the head back. Feel the stretch on the throat. Bring your focus to *Vishuddhi* chakra.

Pose 3: *Padahastasana* (hand to foot pose) Awareness on *Swadhisthana* Chakra

Focus on the lower abdominal area and bend forward from the hips whilst breathing out. Bring the arms down and place the hands beside the feet. If the hands do not reach the floor then let your arms hang from the shoulders. Bring the forehead as close to the knees as is comfortable, lift the lower abdomen to the back of the body and focus on *Swadhisthana* chakra.

Pose 4: *Ashwa Sanchalanasana* (lunge pose) Awareness on *Ajna* Chakra

Bend the knees; place both hands on the floor beside the feet. Breathe in and take the right leg back as far as is comfortable. Press the left foot and fingertips to the floor. Keep the right leg straight or if this is difficult, lower the right knee to the floor. Lift the head slightly, look into the space between the eyebrows and focus on *Ajna* chakra.

Pose 5: *Adho Mukha Svanasana* (down dog pose) Awareness on *Mooladhara* Chakra

Keep both hands on the floor. Breathe out and step the left foot back beside the right foot. At the same time raise the hips upwards and back, lengthen the spine and lower the head between the arms, with the palms and fingers spread out and the surface of the palms flat on the floor. In the final position raise the tail bone, draw the abdomen to the back of the body and lower the head towards the floor. Focus on the base of the body and *Mooladhara* chakra.

Pose 6: *Ashtangasana* (pose of eight points) Awareness on *Manipura* Chakra

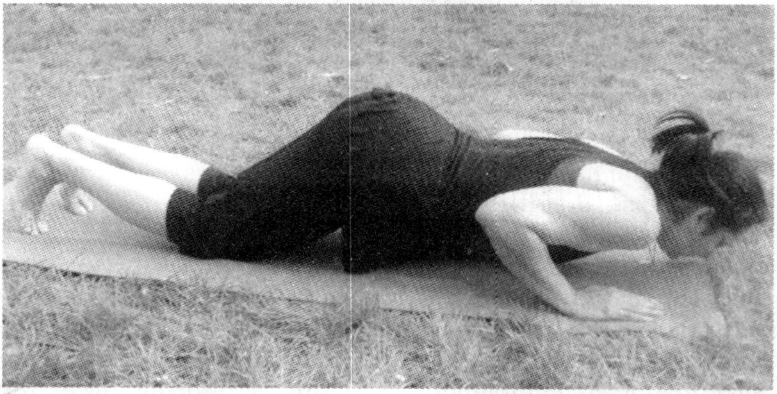

While holding the breath, bring the shoulders forward above the wrists and lower the hips so the body is in a reclining straight line, with the top of the head lengthening to the wall in front and the heels lengthening to the wall behind. Engage the abdominal muscles, then lower the knees to the floor, keep the elbows drawn into the sides of the body as you bend the elbows and lower the chest and chin to the floor, keeping the bottom and the belly lifted. Focus on the mid-abdominal area where *Manipura* chakra is located.

Pose 7: *Bhujangasana* (cobra pose) Awareness on *Swadhisthana* Chakra

Keep the hands on the floor, under the shoulders. Breathe in and raise first the head, then the shoulders and chest. Widen the collar-bones, open the chest as you lengthen the arms, arching the back and drawing the shoulders down away from the ears and the shoulder-blades down the back. Keep the lower abdomen and hips on the floor, and the legs lengthened out behind you. Focus on the lower abdomen and *Swadhisthana* chakra.

Pose 8: *Adho Mukha Svanasana* (down dog pose) Awareness on *Mooladhara* Chakra

Press the palms on the floor, lengthen the arms and whilst exhaling lift the hips up and back, to down dog pose. Keep the feet hip width apart and lower the heels towards the floor, to lengthen the back of the legs. Lift the tailbone, press the whole surface of the palms, fingers and thumbs to the floor and lengthen the arms and sides of the body up and back, whilst lowering the head towards the floor. Keep awareness on the base of the body and *Mooladhara* chakra.

Pose 9: *Ashwa Sanchalanasana* (lunge pose) Awareness on *Ajna* Chakra

From down dog pose, inhale and step the left foot forward and place it between the hands. Keep the right leg straight or place the knee on the floor. Lift the head slightly and look into the space between the eyebrows, focusing on *Ajna* chakra.

Pose 10: *Padahastasana* (hand to foot pose) Awareness on *Swadhisthana* Chakra

From lunge pose, exhale and step the right foot forward next to the left, for forward bend. Keep the legs straight or bend the knees slightly, so the back of the legs do not overstretch. Draw the lower abdomen to the back of the body and the forehead towards the knees. Focus on the lower abdominal area and *Swadhisthana* chakra.

Pose 11: *Hasta Utthanasana* (raised arms pose) Awareness on *Vishuddhi* Chakra

From forward bend, inhale, lengthen and raise the torso and stretch the arms above the head. Keep the arms shoulder width apart and bend back from the hips. Lift the head, arms and upper trunk, bend backwards slightly and open the chest and throat. Keep your focus on the throat area and *Vishuddhi* chakra.

Pose 12: *Prayer pose* (*Pranamasana*) Awareness on *Anahata* Chakra

Breathing out, bring the palms together in front of the chest in prayer pose. Keep the focus on the heart centre and *Anahata* chakra.

This completes a half round. The other half has the following changes:

Pose 4: take your left leg back

Pose 9: bring the right foot between the hands

Sun Salutation *Mantra*

The practice of Sun Salutation is greatly enhanced by chanting a number of *mantras*s which help to keep the mind focused on the physical practice, but also allow us to connect to the power of the sun and give thanks for its significance to the whole earth and to human life. A *mantra* is recited before starting the Sun Salutation and each of the twelve poses in one round of Sun Salutation has its own *mantra*, celebrating different aspects of the sun's power. With practice, the number of rounds builds to twelve and before each round the *mantra* for the corresponding pose is chanted, for example, chant the *mantra* for pose one before beginning round one, the *mantra* for pose two before beginning round two and so on.

The beginning *mantra*, before starting the whole Sun Salutation practice is as follows:

Adi dev numstubhaym Praseed mum bhaskar
Divakar numstubhaym Prabhakar namostute

Meaning: Salutation to the primeval God. Be pleased with me creator of the morning. Creator of day, salutation to you. Creator of light, salutation to you.

The *mantras* for each round and each pose are as follows:

For round one or for the first pose (prayer pose):

Om Mitraya Namaha (Salutation to the friend of all living beings)

For round two or for the second pose (raised arms pose)

Om Ravaye Namaha (Salutation to the glowing one)

For round three or for the third pose (hand to foot pose)

Om Suryaya Namaha (Salutation to Lord Sun)

For round four or for the fourth pose (lunge pose)

Om Bhanave Namaha (Salutation to the glorious one)

For round five or for the fifth pose (down dog pose)

Om Khagaya Namaha (Salutation to the fast mover in the sky)

For round six or for the sixth pose (pose of eight points)

Om Pushne Namaha (Salutation to the provider of power)

For round 7 or for the seventh pose (cobra pose)

Om Hiranya Garbhaya Namaha (Salutation to the golden celestial one)

For round eight or for the eighth pose (down dog pose)

Om Marichaye Namaha (Salutation to the ruler of Dawn)

For round nine or for the ninth pose (lunge pose)

Om Adityaya Namaha (Salutation to the son of Aditi, the celestial mother)

For round ten or for the tenth pose (hand to foot pose)

Om Savitre Namaha (Salutation to the Lord of Creation)

For round eleven or for the eleventh pose (raised arms pose)

Om Arkaya Namaha (Salutation to the one deserving praise)

For round twelve or for the twelfth pose (prayer pose)

Om Bhaskaraya Namaha (Salutation to the giver of enlightenment and wisdom).

17

Restful and Restorative Practice

For a restorative practice, the body is supported and the yoga posture becomes a more passive, relaxing experience with a focus on opening and receiving the breath into particular areas of the body. Combining this with a conscious awareness of the chakra and its' energy, gives an effective, but very restful practice to help balance the whole energy system. Again, this can be a stand alone session or be used to follow the warm-up, the individual chakra practices or the sun salutations. It can also precede or follow chakra breathing and the short chakra meditation practice.

For supported postures you will need several warm blankets, some pillows, a *yoga* bolster (can be purchased at *yoga* equipment suppliers, or fashioned from several blankets rolled together to form a cylinder) and an eye pillow (these can also be purchased at yoga equipment suppliers or can be easily made from smooth material, cut to the shape of an eye mask and filled with uncooked rice).

A quiet, undisturbed space is idea for this practice as each posture is held for up to five minutes. The more simple postures, such as 'child', or 'relaxation' poses may be held for a longer (anything up to ten to fifteen minutes will bring a deep sense of relaxation). With all of the postures begin with up to five minutes, and slowly work up to longer periods of time as the body opens and relaxes. Because the postures are held for longer, ensure you are warm enough and have an extra blanket nearby to put over the body if needed. It can also be helpful to use a clock or timer, so you can decide how long to spend in each of the poses before beginning. Take time to set up the supportive props, experimenting to find the correct height and placement of props to ensure the body feels openness, but no discomfort before settling into the pose.

Supported Child

Child posture is so-called as it is the pose that babies and young children naturally assume when resting. It allows us to connect with a feeling of safety and security, so is well suited to balancing *Mooladhara* energy, as well as relaxing the mind and releasing tension from the lower back and shoulder area.

You will need a yoga bolster, or rolled up blankets. Begin in a kneeling posture with the knees apart. If there is any discomfort in the legs when kneeling, a towel can be folded into the bend of the knees to create more space for the knee-joint, and/or another can be rolled up and placed across the front of the ankles, with the front of the feet hanging over the rolled up area and releasing to the floor.

Place the bolster between the thighs and fold forward over the bolster so the torso is completely supported, allowing the lower back and tail-bone to release towards the floor. The arms can rest around the bolster, to the front, or can rest back towards the feet, with the face turned to one side and the neck lengthened.

Be aware of the breath in the back of the rib-cage and lower back and allow the internal organs and the front of the body to completely relax and release down onto the support beneath.

As you relax, draw the breath further down into the lower back and spine, to the base of the spine. Half-way through, turn the head the other way with the neck lengthened. Allow the body to completely relax and simply be aware of the gentle rise and fall of your breath.

When you are ready to come out of the posture slowly uncurl the spine from the blankets/bolster and gently breathe, before stretching the legs out.

(Do not practice if you are more than three months pregnant, or have chronic back problems).

Supported Bound Angle

This posture allows the pelvis, hips, chest and abdomen to open and relax. It allows us to open to the flow of breath within and to the flow of life, connecting to the fluid quality of *Swadhisthana* chakra. When we breathe fully in this posture the internal organs can receive a plentiful supply of *prana*. The posture is helpful in reducing tension and can also help alleviate menstrual problems.

You will need a bolster or several blankets rolled into a cylinder and some extra pillows or blankets for underneath the knees. Prop the far end of the bolster on top of a yoga block or some firm pillows, so the bolster slopes downwards. Sit in front of the bolster, bend the knees and take the soles of the feet together, allowing the knees to release out to the sides. Place a pillow and blankets underneath the knees and thighs, so the legs can rest comfortably and the hips can relax. Lie back along the bolster and adjust the height of the bolster to ensure the lower back is comfortable and the whole of the spine and head are supported. Place an eye pillow or small towel folded lengthways across the eyes and forehead. Allow the arms to rest out from the body and if needed place a blanket or pillow underneath the forearms.

Rest the back of your body into the support beneath and breathe slowly and evenly, drawing the breath down into the pelvis and lower abdomen. Allow the body to completely relax and simply be aware of the gentle rise and fall of your breath. When you are ready to come out of the posture, slowly draw the knees together, and use your hands to support you to come to upright. Allow the legs and knees to roll to the right, then the left several times to release your hips.

(If there are any lower back, or knee problems, ensure the props are positioned so there is no discomfort, and there is enough support under the thighs to protect the knees. Do not stay too long in the posture).

Simple Supported Backbend

This simple posture allows the belly and abdomen to open, and the ribs to gently lift from the abdominal organs. From this pose we can open the solar plexus and breathe into *Manipura* chakra, feeling the warmth of our breath expanding in the belly.

Simple Supported Backbend

You will need a bolster or several blankets rolled into a cylinder, a pillow and/or folded blanket for underneath the head and an eye pillow or small rolled up towel. Sit with your knees bent and place the bolster widthways behind you and the extra blanket or pillow positioned where your head can be supported.

Lie back, allowing the back of the waist to rest over the bolster, with the buttocks resting on the mat. Rest the back of the head on your pillow and blankets. Ensure the middle of the back is supported, and there is enough height underneath the head and neck to allow the belly to feel open, but not over-stretched. Remain with the knees bent and feet flat on the floor. Arms can rest out at shoulder level, with further blankets underneath, if needed. Place an eye pillow or small towel over the eyes when you are comfortable in the pose. Allow the body to completely relax and simply be aware of the gentle rise and fall of your breath and openness and warmth in the belly.

When ready to come out of the posture, draw the knees to the chest, release the bolster from underneath, rock from side to side to release the lower back, then rest on your side before coming to sit upright.

(Do not practice if there are disc or lower back problems, and lower the height of the support underneath the waist if there is too much of a stretch in the abdomen. Avoid if you are pregnant).

Supported Backbend

Similar to the simple backbend, this posture takes the prop a little higher underneath the back, allowing the body to open more fully in the heart and chest and connecting us to the energy of *Anahata* Chakra.

You will need a bolster, or several blankets rolled into a cylinder, as well as a pillow and/or folded blanket to support the head and another folded blanket or pillow under the knees, as needed. Place the bolster widthways, in line with the base of your shoulder blades and lie back carefully onto the bolster, resting the head on the pillow and folded blanket. Place a rolled up blanket underneath the knees if there is any discomfort in the lower back. Place the palms of the hands on the abdomen. An eye pillow can be placed over the eyes and an extra blanket over the body for warmth, when settled in the pose.

Breathe into the chest and heart, allowing the chest and arm-pit area to open and widen, and feel the heart area soften. Allow the body to completely relax and simply be aware of the gentle rise and fall of your breath in the heart and chest.

To come out of the posture, draw the chin to the throat, use the hands to support you and carefully raise the head to come to upright. Release the bolster from underneath the back, then lie back, draw the knees to the chest, rock from side to side to release the lower back and rest on your side before coming to sit upright.

(Do not practice if you are more than three months pregnant, or have disc or back conditions, such as spondylosis)

Supported Half Shoulderstand

In this pose, we elevate the body, keeping the back of the neck long and the chin drawn in, so we can focus on the throat and connect with the energy of *Vishuddhi* Chakra.

You will need a bolster, or several blankets rolled into a cylinder, some extra folded blankets, a pillow and an eye pillow. You will also need a raised area, such as a chair or sofa, where the lower legs can comfortably lie. Lie down on the floor in front of the raised area, resting the back of the head on a pillow or folded blanket. Lift the hips and place the bolster widthways underneath the lower back, with the last few vertebrae of the spine resting over the edge of the bolster. Lift the lower legs onto the raised area. The body needs to slope downwards towards the neck and throat, so some folded blankets can be placed underneath the ankles and calves to elevate the legs, if needed. Place an eye pillow over the eyes and rest the arms by the sides, palms facing upwards. Place a blanket over the body and another over the feet for warmth, if needed.

Breathe slowly and evenly, aware of the breath passing through the throat. Allow the body to completely relax and simply be aware of the gentle rise and fall of your breath.

To come out of the posture, slowly draw the knees to the chest, release the bolster from underneath, rock from side to side to release the lower back and rest on your side before coming to upright.

(Avoid if you are menstruating or are more than three months pregnant. If the pose creates a feeling of pressure in the head, come out of the posture).

Supported Relaxation

In supported relaxation, we allow the body to completely relax and any last traces of tension to be released. By totally surrendering, we allow the cumulative effects of the whole practice to be experienced and the benefits of restorative *yoga* to work on the body, mind and energy system. When time is short and life seems stressful and busy, it can often feel too difficult to take time for any kind of yoga practice. This is precisely when we need to make time just for relaxation. Even five to ten minutes in the posture will give the body space to de-stress and relieve fatigue and allow the mind some rest and refreshment.

You will need a bolster or several blankets rolled into a cylinder, a cushion or folded blanket under the head and an eye pillow or folded towel over the eyes. An extra blanket over the body for added warmth is advised as the body will cool down as it reaches the deeper stages of relaxation.

Come into the posture slowly, resting the backs of the knees underneath the bolster and the head on the pillow. Place the eye pillow over the eyes and blanket over the body for warmth. Allow the body to rest into the support beneath. Feel the organs of the body soften and allow your inhale to gently deepen and your exhale to slowly lengthen. Feel the brain relaxing, the mind becoming quieter. Simply observe any thoughts passing through the mind without judgement, and let them go. Be aware of tranquillity within and allow the body to completely relax as you focus on the gentle rise and fall of your breath.

To come out of the posture slowly bring movement to the fingers and toes, before bending the knees and drawing the knees to the chest. Place one hand slowly over each knee and gently rock from side to side before rolling to the side to rest, then coming to sit upright.

(If you are more than three months pregnant, lie on your side with the belly supported and a rolled up blanket or bolster to support the top knee, which is bent and lying over and forward of the bottom leg. Change sides half way through. In all cases take time after any restorative posture to recover, before doing anything requiring concentration, such as driving or operating machinery).

18

Meditation on the Chakras

This short meditation works to energise the individual chakras one by one, aided by an associated *mudra* and *bija mantra* which help to activate the chakra's energy. The meditation is ideal after any of the practices in the book, including the warm-up and each of the individual chakra chapters. On it's own it allows a quick 'fine-tuning', of the chakra system. Allow one to two minutes for each chakra when time is short, or five or six minutes for a longer practice.

Begin by sitting in a comfortable posture with the sitting bones gently pressed down. Sit on some folded blankets or a firm pillow to raise the hips if there is discomfort in the lower back.

Awaken the Base Chakra (*Mooladhara*)

- Place the backs of the hands on the knees and join the tips of the thumbs and third fingers together in *Prithivi*, the earth *mudra*. Turn the palms to face downwards.
- Take your focus to the base of the body, breathe gently and evenly and focus on *Mooladhara* energy. Visualise the deep red light at the base of the body becoming clear and balanced as you effortlessly relax. Be aware of a feeling of safeness and security, with all your needs being met, as you softly breathe in and out.
- Take a deep breath in and chant the sound LAM (l-a-u-m) as you exhale, three times.

Awaken the Sacral Chakra (*Swadhisthana*)

- Place the backs of the hands on the knees and join the tips of the thumbs and little fingers together in *Bhudi*, the fluid *mudra*.
- Take your focus to the lower abdominal area and breathe gently and evenly. Focus on *Swadhisthana* energy, a sparkling orange light becoming clear and balanced and allow openness to life and a sense of curiosity, creativity and acceptance to expand within you as you softly breathe in and out.
- Take a deep breath in and chant VAM (pronounced v-a-u-m) as you exhale, three times.

Awaken the Solar Plexus Chakra (*Manipura*)

- Place the backs of the hands on the knees and join the tips of the index fingers and third fingers to the thumbs, in *Rudra*, the fire *mudra*.
- Focus on the solar plexus and breathe evenly and deeply into the belly and abdomen. Feel an openness and warmth expanding within. Visualise a sparkling yellow ball of light in the belly, becoming clearer and brighter. Connect to and re-claim your personal power and strength as you gently breathe in and out.
- Take a deep breath in and chant RAM (pronounced r-a-u-m) as you exhale, three times.

Awaken the Heart Chakra (*Anahata*)

- Place the backs of the hands on the knees and join the tips of the index fingers and thumbs together in *Gyan*, the air *mudra*, the gesture of connecting individual and cosmic consciousness. Place the left hand near the heart, palm facing up and keep the right hand on the knee.
- Keep your focus on the heart area and breathe evenly and gently. Visualise a sparkling emerald green light in the heart area becoming clearer and brighter and focus on feelings of love, kindness and compassion arising in the heart. Allow this warmth and love to be given to yourself, then to other people and finally to the whole

planet. Allow yourself to receive love from the universe, as you softly breathe in and out.

- Take a deep breath in and chant YAM (pronounced y-a-u-m) as you breathe out, three times.

Awaken the Throat Chakra (*Vishuddhi*)

- Place the backs of the hands on the knees and join the tips of the thumbs to the pads of the middle fingers, in *Akashi*, the ether, or space *mudra*. Gently place the tip of the tongue on the roof of the mouth, just behind the front teeth and become aware of inner space.
- Keep your focus on the throat area, breathing evenly and gently. Visualise a sky blue light in the throat becoming clearer and brighter, as you focus on clarity of communication, truthfulness, and harmony. Feel the energy of *Vishuddhi* becoming balanced as you gently breathe in and out.
- Take a deep breath in and chant HAM (pronounced h-a-u-m) as you breathe out, three times.

Awaken the Brow Chakra (*Ajna*)

- Rest the backs of the hands in the lap, with the back of the left hand resting on the right palm and the tips of the thumbs touching, in *Dhyani mudra*, the gesture of meditation.
- Focus on the space between the eyebrows, breathing evenly and gently. Visualise an indigo and lilac light becoming clearer and purer and connect to your inner wisdom and innate judgement, as you softly breathe in and out.
- Take a deep breath in and chant OM (pronounced a-u-m) as you breathe out, three times.

Awaken the Crown Chakra (*Sahasrara*)

- Rest the backs of the hands on the knees and bend the middle fingers to the base of the thumb, then lightly press the middle fingers down with the thumbs, in *Shunya*, the heavenly *mudra*.

- Take awareness to the crown of the head and breathe gently and evenly. Visualise violet light with flashes of pure, sparkling white light becoming clearer and brighter. Focus on your inter-connectedness to all living things, to your higher self and to universal consciousness. Place your trust in this higher consciousness as you softly breathe in and out.
- Take a deep breath in and silently chant *OM* (pronounced a-u-m) as you breathe out, three times.

Sit quietly for a few minutes, breathing gently. Focus on the whole body, mind and energy system becoming balanced and harmonised. Visualise your energy body clear and shining within and connect to the qualities of the chakras-security, creativity, strength, love, gratitude, clarity, peacefulness, wisdom, joy and serenity.

Further Reading

Our book is a basic introduction to the chakras. To deepen your understanding of the chakras and the practise of yoga and meditation, we recommend the following books for further reading.

Ambikananda, Swami Saraswati, Healing Yoga; A Guide to Integrating the Chakras with your Yoga Practise, Connections Book Publishing, London, UK, 2001.

Hirschi, Gertrude, Mudras; Yoga in your Hands, Red Wheel, California, USA, 2000.

Iyengar, B.K.S., Yoga, the Path to Holistic Health, Penguin Group, London, UK, 2001.

Muktibodhananda, Swami, *Swara* Yoga, Yoga Publications Trust, Bihar, India, 1999.

Myss, Caroline, Anatomy of the Spirit; The Seven stages of Power and Healing, Three Rivers Press, London, UK, 1997.

Saradananda, Swami, The Essential Guide to Chakras, Watkins Publishing, London, UK, 2011.

Saradananda, Swami, Chakra Meditation, Duncan Baird Publishers, London, USA, 2008.

Satchidananda, Sri Swami, The Yoga Sutras of Patanjali, Integral Yoga Publications, Virginia, USA, 1978.

Satyananda, Swami Saraswati, Asana, Pranayama, Mudra, Bandha, Yoga Publications Trust, Bihar, India, 1996.

Virtue, Doreen, Chakra Clearing, Awakening Your Power to Know and Heal, Hay House, California, USA, 1998.